The Death Penalty

OPPOSING
VIEWPOINTS®
DIGESTS

The Death Penalty

GAIL B. STEWART

Greenhaven Press Inc., San Diego, California

No part of this book may be reproduced or used in any form or by any means, electrical, mechanical, or otherwise, including, but not limited to, photocopy, recording, or any information storage and retrieval system, without prior written permission from the publisher.

Every effort has been made to trace owners of copyrighted material.

Library of Congress Cataloging-in-Publication Data

Stewart, Gail, 1949–
    The death penalty / Gail B. Stewart.
        p.   cm. — (Opposing viewpoints digests)
    Includes bibliographical references and index.
    Summary: Reviews opposing arguments regarding the death penalty, including whether or not it is just, deters murder, and is applied fairly.
    ISBN 1-56510-744-6 (pbk. : alk. paper). — ISBN 1-56510-745-4 (lib. : alk. paper)
    1. Capital punishment—Moral and ethical aspects—United States—Juvenile literature. 2. Discrimination in capital punishment—United States—Juvenile literature. [1. Capital punishment.] I. Title. II. Series.
HV8699.U5S75   1998
364.66—dc21   97-47685
                                                                    CIP
                                                                    AC

Cover Photo: Superstock
Archive Photos: 21
Library of Congress: 9, 26, 58

©1998 by Greenhaven Press, Inc.
PO Box 289009, San Diego, CA 92198-9009

Printed in the U.S.A.

CONTENTS

FOREWORD

The only way in which a human being can make some approach to knowing the whole of a subject is by hearing what can be said about it by persons of every variety of opinion and studying all modes in which it can be looked at by every character of mind. No wise man ever acquired his wisdom in any mode but this.

—John Stuart Mill

Today, young adults are inundated with a wide variety of points of view on an equally wide spectrum of subjects. Often overshadowing traditional books and newspapers as forums for these views are a host of broadcast, print, and electronic media, including television news and entertainment programs, talk shows, and commercials; radio talk shows and call-in lines; movies, home videos, and compact discs; magazines and supermarket tabloids; and the increasingly popular and influential Internet.

For teenagers, this multiplicity of sources, ideas, and opinions can be both positive and negative. On the one hand, a wealth of useful, interesting, and enlightening information is readily available virtually at their fingertips, underscoring the need for teens to recognize and consider a wide range of views besides their own. As Mark Twain put it, "It were not best that we should all think alike; it is difference of opinion that makes horse races." On the other hand, the range of opinions on a given subject is often too wide to absorb and analyze easily. Trying to keep up with, sort out, and form personal opinions from such a barrage can be daunting for anyone, let alone young people who have not yet acquired effective critical judgment skills.

Moreover, to the task of evaluating this assortment of impersonal information, many teenagers bring firsthand experience of serious and emotionally charged social and health problems, including divorce, family violence, alcoholism and drug abuse, rape, unwanted pregnancy, the spread of AIDS, and eating disorders. Teens are often forced to deal with these problems before they are capable of objective opinion based on reason and judgment. All too often, teens' response to these deep personal issues is impulsive rather than carefully considered.

Greenhaven Press's Opposing Viewpoints Digests are designed to aid in examining important current issues in a way that develops critical thinking and evaluating skills. Each book presents thought-provoking argument and stimulating debate on a single issue. By examining an issue from many different points of view, readers come to realize its complexity and acknowledge the validity of opposing opinions. This insight is especially helpful in writing reports, research papers, and persuasive essays, when students must competently address common objections and controversies related to their topic. In addition, examination of the diverse mix of opinions in each volume challenges readers to question their own strongly held opinions and assumptions. While the point of such examination is not to change readers' minds, examining views that oppose their own will certainly deepen their own knowledge of the issue and help them realize exactly why they hold the opinion they do.

The Opposing Viewpoint Digests offer a number of unique features that sharpen young readers' critical thinking and reading skills. To assure an appropriate and consistent reading level for young adults, all essays in each volume are written by a single author. Each essay heavily quotes readable primary sources that are fully cited to allow for further research and documentation. Thus, primary sources are introduced in a context to enhance comprehension.

In addition, each volume includes extensive research tools. A section containing relevant source material includes interviews, excerpts from original research, and the opinions of prominent spokespersons. A "facts about" section allows students to peruse relevant facts and statistics; these statistics are also fully cited, allowing students to question and analyze the credibility of the source. Two bibliographies, one for young adults and one listing the author's sources, are also included; both are annotated to guide student research. Finally, a comprehensive index allows students to scan and locate content efficiently.

Greenhaven's Opposing Viewpoints Digests, like Greenhaven's higher level and critically acclaimed Opposing Viewpoints Series, have been developed around the concept that an awareness and appreciation for the complexity of seemingly simple issues is particularly important in a democratic society. In a democracy, the common good is often, and very appropriately, decided by open debate of widely varying views. As one of our democracy's greatest advocates, Thomas Jefferson, observed, "Difference of opinion leads to inquiry, and inquiry to truth." It is to this principle that Opposing Viewpoints Digests are dedicated.

A Short History of the Death Penalty

Few issues in the United States today are as emotionally charged and controversial as the death penalty. More formally known as capital punishment, the death penalty has been hotly debated not only as a legal issue, but as a religious, ethical, and political one, historically as well as in the present day.

The death penalty has been a legalized punishment since the time of the Babylonian king Hammurabi between 1760 and 1750 B.C.

Interestingly, the crimes for which the death penalty was deemed proper have changed a great deal over the centuries. In ancient Greece one could be condemned to death for what are today considered very minor crimes—stealing a piece of fruit, for example, or being lazy. In ancient Rome, one who stole another's crops or who disturbed the peace at night could be executed. In the time of Hammurabi (whose code of laws is believed to be the oldest surviving), one could be put to death for murder, robbery, and adultery. And in biblical accounts, acting in God's behalf, Moses proclaimed the death penalty for kidnapping and cursing at one's parents.

By the Middle Ages, England had a large number of crimes for which the death penalty was reserved: murder, treason, petty treason, theft, robbery, burglary, rape, and arson. As time went on, the list of such crimes, known as capital crimes, grew dramatically. By the 1600s, 200 offenses were punishable by death; by 1780, the list, known in Britain as the Bloody Code, had grown to 350.

In a seventeenth-century European town square, a condemned criminal is executed by drawing and quartering. When the horses have stretched his limbs taut, the swordsman hacks them off one by one. Such cruel methods of execution were still in use as recently as the mid–nineteenth century.

Harsh Methods

While the modern trend is toward more humane methods of execution, such as lethal injection, the ancient rule of thumb seemed to be the bloodier and more painful, the better. For example, the Old Testament mentions stoning as a preferred way of executing disobedient children: "If a man have a stubborn and rebellious son, which will not obey the voice of his father, or the voice of his mother" the father may bring his son before the wise men of the city, and the wise men "shall stone him with stones, that he die."[1] Death by stoning was also prescribed for a bride whose husband discovers she is not a virgin on their wedding night.

And stoning was by no means the worst of the early executions. Convicted criminals were burned at the stake, drowned, and crucified. Some were slowly and excruciatingly tortured to death in the practice known as drawing and quartering, as described in this sentence handed down to seven Englishmen convicted of treason in 1812:

> That you and each of you, be taken to the place from whence you came, and from thence be drawn on a hurdle to the place of execution, where you shall be hanged by the neck not till you are dead, but that you be severally taken down, while yet alive, and your bowels be taken out and burned before your faces—that your heads be then cut off, and your bodies cut into four quarters, to be at the King's disposal. And God have mercy on your souls.[2]

Evidence suggests that past societies were not hesitant to enforce their death penalty laws, either. During the first half of the sixteenth century in England, more than seventy-two thousand prisoners were executed, many of them children. Little or no distinction was made in times past between a condemned prisoner who was seven or eight and one who was thirty.

Women, too, were executed in great numbers in England and elsewhere in Europe—on suspicion of witchcraft. By the seventeenth century, more than two hundred thousand women believed to be witches were executed.

Public Displays and Blood Lust?

Executions in the past were always public, in the belief that witnessing the ultimate punishment would deter others from committing the wrongdoer's crimes. The public executions had a carnival-like atmosphere, with townspeople arriving early to get a good view. Families often made a day of it, bringing picnic lunches while they waited for the condemned to be led to the gallows, the stake, the guillotine.

Although deterrence was the alleged reason for the public displays, many historians doubt the value of moral lessons learned on occasions "where thieves and pickpockets joined the other onlookers in merriment."[3] Indeed, the "merriment" more often than not had a tinge of the sadistic, as people seemed all too eager for blood and pain.

Consider the case of Robert-François Damiens, convicted in 1757 of trying to assassinate King Louis XV of France by stabbing. The French court decreed that

> his chest, arms, thighs, and calves be burnt with pincers; his right hand, holding the knife with which he committed [the crime] burnt in sulfur; that boiling oil, melted lead, and rosin and wax mixed with the sulfur be poured in his wounds; and after that his body be pulled and dismembered by four horses, and the members and body consumed in fire, and ashes scattered to the winds.[4]

Damiens's execution date was highly publicized, and mobs of men, women, and children flocked to the site; "[they] gathered in the plaza and on rooftops to watch the torture and to see the horses tear his body asunder."[5] This was not an isolated incident; in 1807 more than forty thousand people gathered to watch a hanging in England. Historians say that the crowd's excitement reached such a peak that dozens of people were trampled to death.

The argument that deterrence was the reason for executions did not seem a strong one. It was, comments one modern writer, as if "in the midst of what was considered at the time to be the pinnacle of civilization, the primitive lust for blood had risen up and consumed the population."[6]

The Death Penalty Comes to America

From its beginning, America included the death penalty in the legal punishments as part of its criminal justice system, which was modeled on England's. As one historian writes, "The criminal law developed here was little more than a series of variations, colony by colony, on the law of . . . the mother country."[7] But although the colonists did adopt a rather scary-sounding collection of capital offenses, many sentences were a paper threat only. For instance, even though cursing one's parent was punishable by death in Massachusetts, no one in America was executed for the offense as they were in England.

Not all of the colonies were eager to keep capital laws on their books, however. In Pennsylvania, the pacifist Quakers did not permit the taking of life as a punishment for any crime except murder and treason.

Early Opposition to the Death Penalty

Although the founders of the new country were generally in favor of the death penalty for certain crimes, many Americans in the late eighteenth and early nineteenth centuries were highly vocal opponents, known as abolitionists.

The best known of the American abolitionists was Dr. Benjamin Rush, a signer of the Declaration of Independence and a confidant of Benjamin Franklin. Like many other Americans at the time, Rush equated the death penalty with a cruel monarchy, specifically that of England's King George, and believed that the new republic should have nothing to do with executions.

Rush wrote a number of pamphlets and books arguing that the very idea of a death penalty contradicted the notion of humanity and divine love. Who are we, he reasoned, to destroy what God has made? Far better to reform a criminal than to destroy him. And what more effective way of reforming him, he reasoned, than by forcing him to reflect on his crime:

> Company, conversation, and even business are the opiates of the Spirit of God in the human heart. For this reason, a bad man should be left for some time without anything to employ his hands in his confinement. Every *thought* should recoil wholly upon *himself*. . . . A wheelbarrow, a whipping post, nay even a gibbet [gallows] are all light punishments compared with letting a man's conscience loose upon him in solitude.[8]

Rush was influential in his home state of Pennsylvania; other leaders joined his abolitionist efforts. By 1830 the movement had spread to a number of other states, which either banned capital punishment altogether or greatly limited the number of capital crimes.

Capital Punishment in and out of Favor

Although the early successes of the abolitionist movement were gratifying to its leaders, the American people continued to seesaw on the issue of the death penalty. For instance, in the late 1800s, Colorado, Iowa, and Kansas all experimented with abolition. Their state legislatures went back and forth between reason and passion. As one source explains, "Reason would persuade them to outlaw capital punishment; then a heinous crime would be committed, and then passion would drive public debate and the death penalty would be reinstated."[9]

During the nineteenth century, executions in the United States were still largely public, as they had been in Europe. People seemed fascinated by execution. For instance, the execution of a man named Sam Steenburgh on April 19, 1878, attracted about fifteen thousand spectators to the little town of Fonda, New York. As one historian writes, "Two special trains from the east, aggregating twelve cars, and one of seven cars, from the west" were needed for people whose ages ranged "from the . . . bent old man or woman of 70 to the child in arms."[10]

But factors other than a carnival-like atmosphere accounted for the popularity of many executions. It seemed when crime numbers were up, or if the economy was in a slump, public sentiment in favor of the death penalty grew. Such wavering made life difficult for politicians who tried to gauge public opinion in states such as Maine, for example. Though Maine abolished the death penalty after the Civil War, its voters changed their minds shortly afterward due to increased crime. Lawmakers did as their constituents demanded, and put the death penalty back on the books. But two decades later, with a steady economy and relatively low crime rate, the public demanded it be abolished once more.

Painless and Swift

Although public opinion has shifted on the question of the death penalty, one trend that has been consistent since the late 1800s is to make executions less brutal. Hanging, for example, has become increasingly unpopular as a method of execution. Historians say that late-nineteenth-century executions were the responsibility of local sheriffs, who were not always proficient as hangmen. The result was that

> the poor devil who'd been sentenced to hang by the neck until dead might do just that. Instead of having his neck vertebrae neatly snapped the instant he fell through the trap, he might twist and turn at the end of the rope for twenty or thirty minutes as life was painfully choked out of him. Or, if he didn't strangle to death, he might suffer the other extreme: the force of the fall might rip off his head, and the witnesses might feel his warm blood spattering over them like rain.[11]

In 1885 David B. Hill, the newly elected governor of New York, spoke for many of his constituents when he called for scientists to come up with a better, more humane method of execution. "The present mode of executing criminals by hanging," he said, "has come down to us from the Dark Ages."[12]

Two hundred scientists, judges, and doctors replied to a questionnaire on the issue; some suggested the quick, painless guillotine, which was rejected by the New York legislature as too bloody. Another suggestion was an overdose of morphine; this method, too, was rejected, because doctors feared that the public might equate morphine with poison and would be alarmed when doctors administered it to them as a painkiller.

The third suggestion was to use high charges of electricity to execute the condemned, and eventually this punishment was approved by the legislature. The electric chair was used for the first time in 1890. Since then other methods, the gas chamber and lethal injection, were developed to make executions less barbaric and painful to the condemned, but abolitionists nevertheless point to instances where prisoners have suffered a great deal regardless of method.

Cruel and Unusual?

Between 1930 and 1967 a total of 3,859 people were executed in the United States. Meanwhile, even with the more modern methods used in carrying out the death penalty, the abolitionist movement was becoming stronger and more vocal. Groups such as the American League to Abolish Capital Punishment worked hard in Washington, D.C., and assorted state legislatures, trying to convince lawmakers to strike the death penalty from the law books.

In the early 1960s, however, the site of the battle over capital punishment changed. Groups such as the American Civil Liberties Union and the Legal Defense Fund, an arm of the National Association for the Advancement of Colored People (NAACP), began challenging capital cases in court, appealing numerous sentences to the Supreme Court.

These abolitionist suits were filed against the two states with the most inmates on death row, Florida and California, on constitutional grounds. The suits claimed that the death penalty violated the Eighth Amendment, which prohibited "cruel and unusual punishment." The lawsuits were successful in that they froze all scheduled executions until the Court could reach a verdict.

Furman vs. Georgia

The most important case, *Furman vs. Georgia*, was decided in 1972. In the *Furman* case, the defense counsel claimed that "as the statutes are administered . . . the imposition and carrying out of the death penalty [constitutes] cruel and unusual punishment."[13] The Supreme Court justices, in a 5-4 decision, agreed that *as it was currently imposed and administered*, the death penalty was not constitutional, that it was too arbitrarily and randomly applied. Justice Potter Stewart, writing for the majority, commented:

> These death sentences are cruel and unusual in the same way that being struck by lightning is cruel and unusual. For of all the people convicted of rapes and murders . . . many just as reprehensible as these, the petitioners are among a capriciously selected random handful upon whom the sentence of death has in fact been imposed.[14]

Justice William O. Douglas concurred, pointing out that minorities are unfairly targeted when death sentences are handed out. The penalty is selectively applied, he wrote,

> feeding prejudices against the accused if he is poor and despised, lacking political clout, or if he is a member of a suspect or unpopular minority, and saving those who by social position may be in a more protected position.[15]

Capital punishment was dealt a severe blow by the Supreme Court in the *Furman* case, but it was not dead. The Court declared a moratorium on further executions, giving the states an opportunity to devise ways to eliminate discrimination from death penalty statutes. If the Court could be persuaded that criteria for deciding who should be executed were unbiased and fairly applied, the death penalty could once again be used. Four years after *Furman*, in *Gregg vs. Georgia*, the Court ruled that new state statutes included sufficient safeguards to make the death penalty constitutionally acceptable. In 1977 murderer Gary Gilmore became the first American in ten years to be executed.

The Debate Rages On

As of 1997 thirty-eight states allow the death penalty. The remaining twelve states and the District of Columbia do not. No serious challenge to the constitutionality of capital pun-

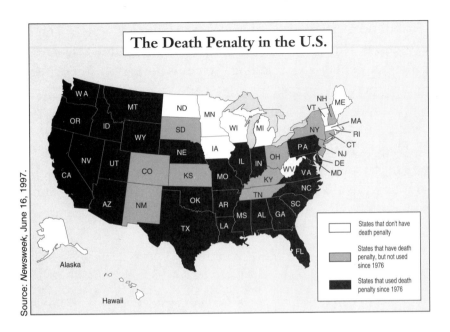

The Death Penalty in the U.S.

Source: *Newsweek*, June 16, 1997.

Legend:
- States that don't have death penalty
- States that have death penalty, but not used since 1976
- States that used death penalty since 1976

ishment appears likely at present, in part because today's Supreme Court is a less liberal body than it was in 1972.

Even so, the debate over the death penalty in the United States is as vigorous and impassioned as it has ever been. Frustrated by what they perceive as an increase in urban street crime—especially the vicious murders related to the drug trade—many Americans are speaking out for the death penalty. Polls indicate that as many as 75 percent of Americans believe that the death penalty is appropriate in some cases.

However, it is also true that many people support death sentencing because they have lost confidence in alternatives such as life sentences. So many prisoners are paroled early that "life in prison" doesn't mean what it says. As Georgia Supreme Court judge Charles Weltner once remarked, "Everybody believes that a person sentenced to life for murder will be walking the streets within seven years."[16] The results of such polls would be far different, say abolitionists, if the option of the verdict of life without possibility of parole was available to juries.

Abolitionists are as vocal as death penalty advocates. Their objections are varied: The death penalty, they insist, violates religious beliefs about killing, remains unfair to minorities and is therefore unconstitutional, and is inhumane and barbaric. They disagree that the death penalty is a deterrent to crime, and worry that innocent people may be executed.

The questions both groups raise are valid ones, and worthy of sincere and thoughtful consideration. The essays that follow provide a context for discussing many of the issues surrounding the use of the death penalty.

1. Quoted in Robert H. Loeb Jr., *Crime and Capital Punishment*. New York: Franklin Watts, 1986, p. 18.

2. Quoted in Loeb, *Crime and Capital Punishment*, p. 21.

3. Loeb, *Crime and Capital Punishment*, p. 27.

4. Quoted in Jesse Jackson, *Legal Lynching: Racism, Injustice, and the Death Penalty*. New York: Marlowe, 1996, pp. 31–32.

5. Jackson, *Legal Lynching*, p. 32.

6. Jackson, *Legal Lynching*, p. 32.

7. Hugo Adam Bedau, ed., *The Death Penalty in America: Current Controversies*. New York: Oxford University Press, 1997, p. 3.

8. Quoted in David Freeman Hawke, *Benjamin Rush: Revolutionary Gadfly*. Indianapolis: Bobbs-Merrill, 1971, p. 366.

9. Jackson, *Legal Lynching*, p. 37.

10. Quoted in Lawrence M. Friedman, *Crime and Punishment in American History*. New York: BasicBooks, 1993, pp. 168–69.

11. Frederick Drimmer, *Until You Are Dead: The Book of Executions in America*. New York: Citadel, 1990, p. 9.

12. Quoted in Drimmer, *Until You Are Dead*, p. 9.

13. Quoted in Mark Siegel, Carol Foster, and Nancy Jacobs, eds., *Capital Punishment*. Wylie, TX: Information Aids, 1988, p. 4.

14. Quoted in Siegel, Foster, and Jacobs, *Capital Punishment*, p. 5.

15. Quoted in Burt Henson and Ross R. Olney, *Furman v. Georgia: The Constitution and the Death Penalty*. New York: Franklin Watts, 1996, pp. 73–74.

16. Quoted in Jackson, *Legal Lynching*, p. 56.

CHAPTER 1

Is the Death Penalty Just?

"In the Constitution . . . the legality of taking a criminal's life is not only mentioned but assumed."

The Death Penalty Is Legally Just

Parts of the criminal justice system are straightforward, requiring little interpretation or subjective thinking to understand their meaning. For instance, law enforcement officials must properly collect and introduce evidence to determine whether a suspect did in fact commit a crime. And once a suspect is apprehended, very clear rules are followed on the process of his or her arrest. Crimes themselves are clearly defined, as well: murder, arson, robbery.

Where things get muddy is in the sentencing of criminals, which spills over into the areas of ethics and morality. The death penalty, certainly the most severe of sentences, has long been the topic of passionate, emotionally charged arguments. It has been left to the courts, especially the Supreme Court, to decide whether death is a suitable, appropriate penalty in certain instances under our laws.

A Long History

The death penalty in the United States has a long, if not illustrious, history. It is not something recently proposed; indeed, penalty by death was legally sanctioned before the colonies won their independence.

The laws of England, which applied to the American colonies, permitted executions for fourteen different crimes, including swearing, perjury, arson, worshiping idols, adultery, murder, and practicing witchcraft. Opponents of these laws included the Quakers, who were against the taking of life under any circumstances, and Dr. Benjamin Rush, a contemporary of Benjamin Franklin. Rush, considered the founder of the abolitionist movement, wrote many influential books attacking the death penalty. In 1790 Rush wrote that the death penalty was more properly associated with tyranny than with a free republic. Republics, he wrote, "appreciate human life. . . . They consider human sacrifices . . . offensive."[1] In the late eighteenth century, however, the death penalty was still socially acceptable.

Benjamin Rush

Now, most opponents of the death penalty are fond of quoting the Eighth Amendment to the Constitution, the one that forbids "cruel and unusual" punishment. According to them, the death penalty is cruel and unusual, and therefore unconstitutional. But read the Constitution more carefully, and you'll find that the death penalty is mentioned. It bears repeating, since that fact is paramount in any discussion of the constitutionality of the death penalty: It is mentioned in the Constitution itself—twice. Twice the legality of taking a criminal's life is not only mentioned but *assumed*.

The first occurrence is in the Fifth Amendment of the Bill of Rights, which states that "no person shall be held to answer for a capital . . . crime, unless on a presentment or indictment of a Grand Jury . . . nor be deprived of life . . . without due process of law." In other words, the Constitution is specifying that the death penalty may be used, but warns that there are certain stipulations that must first be met.

Additionally the Fourteenth Amendment says that states shall not "deprive any person of life, liberty, or property, without due process of law." Again, the idea of the death penalty—depriving a person of his or her life—is not the issue here. That much is assumed. The purpose of the amendment is to guarantee that the individual has the same protection under state laws as he or she does under the Bill of Rights. The phrase "due process of law" may be subject to debate, but surely not the idea that the individual can, under some circumstances, be deprived of life. The only question here is the process by which that can be accomplished.

Attention to Injustice

Knowing that the founders were concerned about the fair application of the death penalty, not the existence of the death penalty, it is important to understand how hard we as Americans have worked to make sure that the death penalty *in practice* works justly.

Throughout the history of the United States movements have attempted to abolish the death penalty on legal grounds. In 1972, for example, in *Furman vs. Georgia*, the Supreme Court ruled that *as it was currently used*, the death penalty did violate a constitutional ban on "cruel and unusual" punishments. The justices were convinced that although punishment by death was not an uncommon sentence, executions were rarely carried out. In Justice Potter Stewart's opinion,

> These death sentences are cruel and unusual in the same way that being struck by lightning is cruel and unusual. For of all the people convicted of rapes and murders . . . many just as reprehensible as these, the petitioners are among a capriciously selected random handful upon whom the sentence of death has in fact been imposed. . . . I simply conclude that the 8th and 14th amendments cannot tolerate the infliction of a sentence of death under legal systems that

permit this unique penalty to be so wantonly and so freakishly imposed.[2]

This 5-4 decision by the Supreme Court was not an end to capital punishment, only to the arbitrary way in which it was applied. The death penalty must be imposed fairly, said the Court, or not at all. Therefore, when in 1976 a new case came to the Supreme Court (*Gregg vs. Georgia*) and the justices were convinced that the arbitrariness that had existed in the past had been rectified, they allowed the death penalty, stating, "The infliction of death as a punishment for murder is not without justification and . . . is not unconstitutionally severe."[3]

Without a Legal Question

Since the *Furman* decision, the Supreme Court has made every possible effort to make the death penalty fair. It has demanded balance and consistency. It has demanded equality and fairness.

The Constitution is only a framework. Because the death penalty is mentioned does not mean that it *must* be used—indeed, some states have abolished the death penalty. Although today an estimated 75 percent of Americans favor the death penalty, it is certainly true that the day may come when the tide will turn. We may someday decide that executions under any circumstances are inherently inhumane. If that were to happen, it is still important to keep in mind that the death penalty's abolition would take place on moral grounds, and would have nothing to do with its constitutionality.

1. Quoted in Lawrence M. Friedman, *Crime and Punishment in American History*. New York: BasicBooks, 1993, p. 74.

2. Quoted in Burt Henson and Ross R. Olney, *Furman v. Georgia: The Constitution and the Death Penalty*. New York: Franklin Watts, 1996, pp. 74–75.

3. Quoted in JoAnn Bren Guernsey, *Should We Have Capital Punishment?* Minneapolis: Lerner Publications, 1993, p. 13.

"The wrongness of the death penalty in the United States is simply a point of law, and a quick, thoughtful reference to the Constitution will clear up any confusion."

The Death Penalty Is Legally Unjust

There are all kinds of reasons for people to disagree about the rightness or wrongness of the death penalty in America. Some make it a religious issue, declaring their position superior and substantiating it by quoting verses in the Bible or other holy texts. Others make the death penalty a philosophical or moral debate, posing such weighty questions as, "What is the true value of human life?" or, "Can governments decide life-and-death issues for individuals?"

But while such debates might be interesting, they would surely become mired in minute details that could never be agreed upon by both sides. I propose that the wrongness of the death penalty in the United States is simply a point of law, and a quick, thoughtful reference to the Constitution will clear up any confusion.

The Eighth Amendment to that document, part of the Bill of Rights, addresses the treatment of prisoners. It states: "Excessive bail shall not be required, nor excessive fines imposed, nor cruel and unusual punishments inflicted." Of these sixteen words, the three most often cited as proof that the death penalty is unconstitutional are "cruel and unusual." In other words, if the Supreme Court should decide that the death penalty is cruel and unusual, then it would be deemed unconstitutional, and scrapped.

Nothing Written in Stone

Proponents of the death penalty would say—quite correctly—that the Supreme Court has looked at the Eighth Amendment and ruled that "cruel and unusual" did not pertain to the death penalty. However, it is important to understand that even though the justices of a former Court might have disagreed that executions were cruel and unusual, this fact does not mean that the Supreme Court in the future may rule the opposite. Law in the United States is not written in stone; although the words are static, the interpretation of them is certainly not. As one legal expert has pointed out, "At any time, the Constitution means what the Supreme Court says it means."[1] And as we near the twenty-first century, it is certain that the American people will reexamine how we look at the death penalty.

There is no doubt that society has changed its views of the notion of cruelty over the years. Consider this description of an execution in 1379 of a man accused of disturbing the peace the night before:

> The prisoner catches sight of the gallows. He cries out and resists his captors but is slapped into submission and pushed toward one of the two ladders. He climbs up; the hangman on the ladder next to him slips the rope around his neck. At the top, the rope is fastened around a horizontal beam. The hangman descends his ladder and kicks the prisoner's ladder out from under him. There is a snap, and then a choking sound comes from the condemned man. The hangman climbs back up, reaches over, and cuts him down. The man's body plops onto the ground. The hangman descends his ladder, produces a sharp knife, lifts the man's tunic, and deftly disembowels him on the spot. As his entrails spill out, they

are gathered up and tossed into a fire. With an ax the executioner severs the man's head from his body.[2]

Over the course of more than six hundred years, humankind has moved from drawing and quartering prisoners to beheading them, from shooting them by firing squads to hanging them. These changes were motivated by a desire to be more humane, more merciful. And so when we became uncomfortable with hanging (because of the possibility that if the drop was too short the victim's neck would not be broken, and if too long, the head would be severed from the body), we turned to modern technology to supply us with the electric chair.

It was hoped that the electric chair, introduced in 1890, would do what other methods of execution had not done—provide a quick, humane death. The *New York Times* hailed its arrival, proclaiming, "This is a step forward in the cause of humanity."[3] However, such lofty praise was misplaced.

The electric chair was introduced in 1890 to modernize and humanize such past methods of execution as drawing and quartering, shooting by a firing squad, and hanging.

Tales abound of flesh burning, flames leaping out of the heads and legs of victims, and eyeballs popping out of their sockets. After one such execution, one witness snorted when asked if this method were as merciful as it was intended to be, "I'd rather see ten hangings. It was fearful. No humane man could witness it without the keenest agony."[4]

Most other witnesses agree—even prison wardens and chaplains for whom such occurrences are a part of their work. If such methods were used on animals, for example, they would be declared criminal. In 1995, for example, the American Veterinary Medical Association (AVMA) brought charges against California chinchilla farmers because they electrocute their animals as a "humane" method of killing them. New guidelines by the AVMA now require animals to be rendered unconscious before being jolted—something we've yet to do to our human victims. So much for mercy and humanity.

"Degrading to Human Dignity"

The latest innovation, death by lethal injection, is no less gruesome than Old Sparky (as the electric chair is known in many prisons). In one out of four cases, executioners have difficulty finding a suitable vein for the injection, and a bloody procedure called a venous cutdown is necessary to place the injection apparatus. In one execution in 1985, it took more than forty minutes for officials to pierce a vein in the victim's body. Or take the case of prisoner Raymond Landry in 1988. "Two minutes into the execution," reports one expert, "the syringe came out of Landry's vein, spraying deadly chemicals across the room toward witnesses. The observation curtain was pulled for fourteen minutes while the execution team reinserted the catheter into the vein."[5]

Such a circuslike atmosphere does nothing to promote mercy and humanity. Indeed, our inability to find a means of killing that is *not* demeaning and cruel proves that the Eighth Amendment is violated every time a prisoner is plucked from death row and strapped into the chair, hanged, or injected with poison.

Supreme Court justice William Brennan believed just that when he condemned capital punishment in a 1972 brief:

> A punishment is cruel and unusual, therefore, if it does not comport with human dignity. . . . Punish-

ment must not by its severity be degrading to human dignity. . . . Death is a unique punishment in the United States. . . . Death is today an unusually severe punishment, unusual in its pain, in its finality, and in its enormity. No other existing punishment is comparable to death in terms of physical and mental suffering.[6]

Though Brennan did not hold the majority view in that 1972 case, his words give hope to those of us who believe that the death penalty cannot last in our society, and that the day will come when it will be abandoned.

1. Nick DiSpoldo, "Capital Punishment and the Poor," *America*, February 11, 1995, p. 8.

2. Donald D. Hook and Lothar Kahn, *Death in the Balance: The Debate over Capital Punishment*. Lexington, MA: Lexington Books, 1989, p. 11.

3. Quoted in Frederick Drimmer, *Until You Are Dead: The Book of Executions in America*. New York: Citadel, 1990, p. 11.

4. Quoted in Drimmer, *Until You Are Dead*, p. 15.

5. Michael Radelet, "Poorly Executed," *Harper's Magazine*, June 1995, pp. 21–22.

6. Quoted in Burt Henson and Ross R. Olney, *Furman v. Georgia: The Constitution and the Death Penalty*. New York: Franklin Watts, 1996, p. 72.

"What is needed . . . is a humane, pain-free, merciful method of death. Such a method does exist."

Executions Can Be Humane

Opinion polls taken in 1997 suggest that America is more in favor of the death penalty than ever before. More than 70 percent of us seem to want the state to dispose of the most brutal criminals in the most final of ways. But while the numbers may seem overwhelming, some experts believe that we may lose our resolve if we knew more about the facts of execution.

There's even a name for this theory—the Marshall Hypothesis, named after former justice Thurgood Marshall. Marshall, a longtime opponent of capital punishment, believed that if Americans knew more about the cruel and inhumane methods of execution, "the great mass of citizens . . . would conclude that the death penalty is immoral and therefore unconstitutional."[1]

What the public needs, then, is to be assured that executions are not inhumane or cruel. Then society could be more resolute in our approval of the death penalty. What is standing in our way? The simple fact that the four main means of execution used today—electrocution, lethal gas, lethal injection, and hanging—*can* occasionally cause pain and suffering.

Not on Purpose

None of these occasional effects is intentional, for that would be cruel and unusual, something our Constitution expressly forbids in the use of the death penalty. For instance, when Mississippi executed Jimmy Lee Gray in the gas chamber in 1983, his head was not immobilized. As the poison gas began suffocating Gray, eyewitnesses and media representatives reported Gray "suffering a torturous death, his head flailing about wildly, smashing the metal pipe [behind his chair, used as a support] many times before he lost consciousness."[2] While no one can say with certainty that the seizures Gray suffered were painful, the spectacle and consequent reporting of his gruesome death made many people squeamish.

The electric chair, and hanging, too, sometimes fail to be quick, and there have been glitches in lethal injections—executioners have sometimes had difficulty finding usable veins into which to inject the poison, and some victims have suffered breathing trauma before being rendered unconscious by the injection. No matter how "clean" our system of execution has been up until now, there are slipups, and these slipups make us nervous.

Perfectly Humane

What is needed, then, is a humane, pain-free, merciful method of death. Such a method does exist—and it was stumbled upon quite by accident in the early days of the Space Shuttle program.

A worker had gone into one of the huge external fuel tanks, unaware that it had just been cleaned with pure nitrogen gas. (Nitrogen gas is used to keep oxygen in the air from corroding the interior of the tank.) After walking just a few yards into the tank, he lost consciousness and collapsed. A fellow worker, not understanding what had happened, ran to his aid, but collapsed as well. In just a short time, the two men died, asphyxiated by nitrogen gas.

A similar accident occurred in California in 1995. Two men had stolen a cylinder of what they believed to be laughing gas from a local hospital. What the cylinder contained, however, was pure nitrogen. As one writer reports:

When the two men stopped their car to partake of their booty, the nitrogen gas displaced the air in the car, leaving them without oxygen. Had they had any indication of the problem, they could have saved their lives simply by opening the car doors.[3]

Why, then, if inhaling nitrogen can produce death so swiftly and painlessly, don't we use it as a humane means of execution? Surely it would be superior to the traumatic deaths sometimes experienced with lethal injection and poison gas used in gas chambers. In his article "Killing with Kindness," Stuart A. Creque describes what death by nitrogen asphyxiation would be like:

> The victim is not racked by a choking sensation or a burning urge to breathe, because as far as his body knows, he is breathing normally, carbon dioxide is not building up in his bloodstream, so he never realizes that anything is wrong, nor does he experience any discomfort; he simply passes out when his blood oxygen falls too low.[4]

In addition to providing a pain-free, nontraumatic death, nitrogen is cheap. Because it is not a toxic chemical, it needs no special environmental precautions for storage or disposal. All in all, it seems a perfect solution to the understandable second thoughts Americans might have on the use of the death penalty.

---

1. Quoted in Hugo Adam Bedau, ed., *The Death Penalty in America: Current Controversies.* New York: Oxford University Press, 1997, p. 101.

2. Donald A. Cabana, *Death at Midnight: The Confessions of an Executioner.* Boston: Northeastern University Press, 1996, p. 7.

3. Stuart A. Creque, "Killing with Kindness," *National Review*, September 11, 1995, p. 52.

4. Creque, "Killing with Kindness," p. 52.

"Before feeling sorry for [the executed], we should remember the real victims . . . who did not have such merciful options."

The Death Penalty Does Not Need to Be Humane

I read a disturbing account recently of an execution that took place in Texas, I think. The man, who had tortured and raped a sixteen-year-old girl before stabbing her to death, was strapped onto a gurney, and the needle containing the lethal dose of whatever-it-is was ready, but the attendants (they can't be doctors, because doctors aren't allowed to kill people legally) couldn't find a good vein.

So they poked, and prodded, and cut, and after twenty or thirty minutes—and after using up a whole lot of cotton balls and alcohol swabs—they were able to find a way to get the show on the road. The story I read was graphic—it described the witnesses' nausea at having to hear the tearful moans of the prisoner and to see the bloodiness of the procedure.

And as I said, the whole thing was really upsetting to me—but not because of the pain suffered by the prisoner. What bothered me was the way in which this "botched" execution was used by the opponents of the death penalty. Words like "vicious" and "barbaric" were used to describe the process. People asked, dumbfounded, "Is *this* the level to which we, as a nation, have sunk?"

Who Is the Victim?

I'm trying to be patient and open-minded, really I am. But I am confused. Why are we talking about a rapist and murderer as a victim? Is our collective memory so short that we have forgotten what real suffering is?

It's not just this one case, either. A year ago, I heard about the painful execution by firing squad of John Albert Taylor, a real prince of a fellow. Described by psychologists as a "remorseless pedophile," Taylor stalked a little eleven-year-old girl named Charla Hill. He attacked her when she was alone in her mother's house. In an ordeal that is believed to have lasted an hour and a half, he tore off her clothes, stuffed her underpants in her mouth, raped her, and strangled her with a telephone cord.

It should be difficult for anyone to work up much sympathy for John Albert Taylor if we are clear about the reasons he was executed before a Utah firing squad in the first place. It wasn't as if by some cruel act of fate he was snatched up and deposited in that courtyard with his hands cuffed, staring down the barrels of all those guns.

Little Charla Hill is the one for whom we should feel sadness. Her family raised her for twelve years. "[They] loved her, cared for her, watched her take her first baby steps, heard her laughter, saw the pictures she painted in school, dreamed of her future as she trembled on the brink of adolescence," writes one reporter. "All of this ended in ninety minutes of misery at the hands of a creature whose continued existence was an affront to humanity."[1]

In the Deep Secret Place of Our Souls

It used to be, not so very long ago, that death was not the worst punishment to which an offender could be sentenced. During the Roman Empire, for instance, criminals were crucified, an excruciatingly painful execution that usually lasted many hours. The fifteenth-century Spanish Inquisition was

The *Wizard of Id* by Brant Parker & Johnny Hart is reprinted by permission of Johnny Hart and Creators Syndicate, Inc., ©1993 by Creators Syndicate, Inc.

also noted for the use of torture for prisoners. The officials of the Inquisition, in fact, had prolonging death down to a science. Consider, for instance, the *potro*, a water torture that involved slowly pouring water over a piece of linen inserted in the throat, forcing the cloth deeper and deeper. As water filtered through the cloth, writes one Spanish historian, "the patient was subjected to all the torments of suffocation, the more cruel because he was driven by his instincts to make futile efforts to ease his condition."[2]

Cruel? Unusual? Without a doubt. And if John Albert Taylor had raped and murdered a little girl four hundred years before, it would have been just what he would have experienced, and not one of us would have blinked an eye.

A few moments of pain or discomfort before death for these criminals does not weigh on my conscience. Before feeling sorry for such a person, we should remember the real victims, people like Charla Hill, who did not have such merciful options.

1. Don Feder, "Pity the Poor Killers, Execution Hurts," *Conservative Chronicle*, February 14, 1996, p. 20.

2. Quoted in Gail B. Stewart, *Life During the Spanish Inquisition*. San Diego: Lucent Books, 1998, p. 71.

"[The death penalty is] a way of giving the victims and their families a feeling of satisfaction . . . , to make them whole . . . or restore integrity."

The Death Penalty Can Ease the Suffering of Victims' Families

When Bonnie Serpico was raped and murdered in 1979, her husband, Andy, was outraged by the way the trial and clemency hearings of her assailant, James Free, were handled by the justice system. He was not allowed to mention to the jury that he and his wife had children—the judge felt it would be prejudicial to the jury. He and his daughters weren't even allowed to sit where the jury could get a good look at them, whereas James Free's mother was allowed to sit right in front of the jury.

The emphasis, fumed Serpico, was not on the victim, and the cruel way she had been killed. Instead, the focus was on the killer. Said Serpico, "Everybody would get to meet James Free, get to know James Free. I wanted people to remember that Bonnie Serpico was a real person."[1]

Recognizing the Pain of a Victim's Family

But in recent years there has been a move toward recognizing the rights of crime victims and their families. It is increasingly common for a tearful family member to address the convicted murderer in court, to be given an opportunity to express the grief and pain resulting from the loss of a wife, a husband, a brother, a daughter. And sixteen states allow victims' families to view executions, the idea being that the victim's loved ones can gain peace of mind through the killer's death.

"We've been trying to sensitize people to the fact that victims should not be considered outsiders in the criminal justice system," explains one activist for victims' rights. "They have a stake; they should be in the forefront. We deserve and demand a place at the table."[2]

Some might argue that such "peace of mind" and having "a place at the table" are merely euphemisms for vengeance—hardly a civilized response in our modern society. However, "vengeance" is not an accurate word; retribution is what society hungers for, at a time when the United States seems to be awash in violent crime. It is not vengeance that victims' families seek—that would be almost impossible.

"My family and I have been characterized as hatemongers for wanting to watch [the execution of her children's murderer]," says one Houston woman. "We are not hatemongers. If we were really bent on revenge, we would have gotten him ourselves at the trial."[3] Indeed, many protest that if they were out only for vengeance, they would be disappointed, for no form of execution today can match the savagery of what murder victims go through. How, for example, can death by lethal injection "equal" the death by raping and strangulation, or the torture of mutilation? Or multiple murder?

Balancing the Scales

No, it isn't merely vengeance, but retribution—a way that society can balance the scales, says Jack Collins, whose daughter was brutally raped, beaten, tortured, and murdered:

> It's a way of giving the victims and their families a
> feeling of satisfaction for what was done to them, to

make them whole as far as possible or restore integrity—the quality or state of completeness—to both the people and the system. Nothing will ever bring Suzanne back to us. But even if this retribution doesn't bring complete closure, it shows us that society, the jury, and the entire criminal justice system care enough about us to see to it that our daughter's killer receives his appropriate punishment. It lets us know that they did right by us as far as they could.[4]

The execution of a killer, while certainly not single-handedly healing the wounds for victims, can certainly be an important step in the process, as Vicki Haack and her family learned recently. In 1986 a crack addict named Kenneth Harris had entered Haack's sister's apartment, raped and choked her, and then spent almost an hour drowning her in the bathtub.

In June 1997, Haack and her family stood in a small viewing room as Harris was strapped to a gurney in the Huntsville, Texas, penitentiary. Haack had rid herself of her rage and hatred of Harris, she says, but she still was in favor of Harris's execution. "We have no hate or bitterness in our hearts," she explains, "but that doesn't mean he does not pay for his crime." The payment, says Haack, was exacted by the state; however, in the moments before he was injected with the lethal chemicals that would kill him, Harris turned to Haack and her family and said, "I hope you can go on with your lives and we can put an end to this."[5]

Honoring a Life

What happens when the punishment goes unserved, or when it is far less severe than the crime? To put a murderer behind bars for a decade or so, a punishment that is effectively the same as an embezzler would get, is disrespectful. It devalues the life that was lost, making a mockery of justice.

Donnetta Apple's brother was killed in the bombing of the Murrah federal building in Oklahoma City. Although never a supporter of the death penalty, Apple feels now that anything less than death would be a slap in the face to her brother and the 167 others who were killed in the bombing. To her, she says, it boils down to the concept of making choices—one of the most important, basic parts of life:

> [Timothy McVeigh] chose to park that truck, put in his earplugs, and walk off. When he did that, he took away the rights of 168 people to ever make decisions of their own again. My brother and the others can't elect to work, or play, or spend time with their families. So I don't want McVeigh to have the freedom to even get a drink of water in his cell. If those 168 victims can't make the most basic of choices, why should he? [He] has to pay for the choice he made on April 19, 1995—and he has to pay with his life.[6]

It is time we paid attention to the victims of the unspeakable crimes that occur in our society. They—more than anyone—understand the pain and loss that such crimes cause. They deserve the healing and closure that can come with resolution. And their voices need to be heard.

1. Quoted in "The Place for Vengeance," *U.S. News & World Report*, June 16, 1997, p. 31.

2. Quoted in John Douglas and Mark Olshaker, *Journey into Darkness*. New York: Scribner, 1997, p. 365.

3. Quoted in "The Place for Vengeance," p. 29.

4. Quoted in Douglas and Olshaker, *Journey into Darkness*, p. 366.

5. Quoted in "The Place for Vengeance," p. 25.

6. Quoted in "The Families Debate McVeigh's Fate," *Newsweek*, June 16, 1997, p. 30.

"An eye for an eye makes the whole world blind."

The Death Penalty Encourages Vengeance, Not Healing

Responding to the Old Testament edict, the great Indian leader Mahatma Gandhi said, "An eye for an eye makes the whole world blind." The notion of justice as retaliation or vengeance, he taught, is a trap of violence.

Such a trap can be found among the current theories about the value of the death penalty as therapeutic for the families of the murder victim. In watching the killer's execution, the thinking goes, the family can experience resolution, closure, and peace. Not only is such thinking flawed, but it is insidious, for it preys upon a small and extremely vulnerable segment of our society.

Pressure on Grieving Families

Often it is prosecutors themselves who stoke a grieving family's rage by trying to convince them that the death penalty will help end their suffering. One woman, whose daughter was murdered in 1980, recalls how dependent she was on the prosecution lawyers:

> When you have lost a child, you go into a state of insanity, and you think whatever they want you to think. They told me, "We are going to catch this man. We're going to convict him, and when we have an execution, you will be healed." The D.A. [district attorney] told me this, and the sheriff's department, also the media. And I believed them.[1]

In fact, some family members of crime victims say that the pressure on grieving families is so strong that *not* to want the killer to receive the death penalty implies that you didn't value the murder victim. Marietta Jaeger, whose seven-year-old daughter was murdered but who opposes the death penalty, appeared on a televised talk show with the Harveys, a couple whose daughter was also murdered. The Harveys were strong supporters of the death penalty, even demonstrating in its favor outside prisons whenever an execution took place.

Marietta talked about how much she loved her daughter, but explained that she couldn't wish for her daughter's murderer to be executed. After the show, Mrs. Harvey said to her, "It's a shame you didn't love your daughter the way we loved ours."[2]

Making Things Worse

Although realizing that feelings of rage and the need for vengeance are natural when a person has experienced such a loss, experts know that those feelings are stages in the grieving process. They are not meant to be sticking points. To stay permanently entrenched in anger and rage is no more healthy than it is to stay in denial, or to cry incessantly.

And feelings of vengeance that can only be quenched by seeing the murderer die in the electric chair or by lethal injection cannot bring about closure. Such emotions cannot do anything but keep the grieving person feeling raw and bitter, for as anyone who understands death penalty laws can attest, the road to executing a convicted killer is usually more than a decade long—if it ever ends. All those court appearances, all those appeals filed—*this* is supposed to bring closure to a hurting family member? In truth, the death penalty causes more pain than other sentences. "The continuous sequence of courtroom scenes inherent in death penalty cases," says Marietta Jaeger, "only serve to keep emotional wounds raw and in pain for years."[3]

Moving Beyond Hate

Other stories seem to substantiate Jaeger's beliefs. Take the case of Sandra Miller, who spent more than sixteen years hating William Bonin, dubbed the Freeway Killer in California. Bonin raped, tortured, and murdered her fifteen-year-old son, Rusty, as well as thirteen other boys. Bonin was finally executed for his crimes in February 1996.

Miller says that she was consumed by rage; on the day of Bonin's execution, she sent him a note: "I think of how I could torture you. You've brought out feelings in me that I didn't know a human being could have."[4] She was certain that the execution would erase those feelings, but it did not. She had spent much of the time since Rusty's death in an alcoholic haze, and was unable to participate in the lives of her other children. "My other two kids lost their brother and then they lost their mother,"[5] she admits.

What helped Miller was not Bonin's death, she says, but getting to know more about Bonin himself, after his execution. In the process of being interviewed for a book about Bonin, she became friends with the biographer. She learned about Bonin's childhood, and some of the factors that created this "monster" who could murder children. She found some compassion, which helped her grieve more fully. As a result, she was able to reach out to the rest of her family.

Those who advocate the death penalty on the grounds that it will somehow avenge the murders the executed person committed are confused. How is the wife, mother, husband, son of a victim supposed to feel, knowing that the state is going to "even the scales" by using lethal injection, gas, or the electric chair? How could such an act even the score?

All that happens is that the cycle of killing continues, without healing or help for any of the victims. In fact, when executions occur, there are new victims—a new set of parents, brothers, sisters, who are grieving. This is what writer Ruth Morris calls "misery justice," a kind of system that never actually makes anyone feel better but, as she says, "just tries to ensure offenders and their families are as miserable as the most miserable victim of crime."[6]

What are we teaching our youngest citizens when the best we can offer is a kind of justice that kills? What kind of help are we giving those grieving the murder of family members when the best we can do is turnabout? Listen, instead, to what Coretta Scott King says about the idea of executing the murderer of her husband, Dr. Martin Luther King:

> Although my husband was assassinated and my mother-in-law was murdered, I refuse to accept the cynical judgment that their killers deserve to be executed. To do so would perpetuate the tragic cycle of violence that feeds itself. It would be a disservice to all that my husband and his mother lived for and believed.[7]

It seems infinitely more important that the victims and their families are honored and valued by a violence-free response to such crimes. Rage and loathing, carried to such an extreme, demeans us all.

1. Quoted in "The Place for Vengeance," *U.S. News & World Report*, June 16, 1997, p. 28.

2. Quoted in George M. Anderson, "Opposing the Death Penalty: An Interview with Helen Prejean," *America*, November 9, 1996, p. 10.

3. Quoted in Jesse Jackson, *Legal Lynching: Racism, Injustice, and the Death Penalty*. New York: Marlowe, 1996, p. 57.

4. Quoted in "The Place for Vengeance," p. 29.

5. Quoted in "The Place for Vengeance," p. 31.

6. Ruth Morris, "Alternatives to the Death Penalty," *Witness*, September 1997, p. 18.

7. Quoted in Jackson, *Legal Lynching*, p. 23.

CHAPTER 2

Does the Death Penalty Deter Murder?

"For every execution that occurred in the United States in the period 1933–1967, between seven and eight potential murders were avoided."

The Death Penalty Deters Murder

In 1975 University of Chicago economist Isaac Ehrlich published a paper in the *American Economic Review* titled "The Deterrent Effect of Capital Punishment: A Question of Life and Death." In his study, Ehrlich found a correlation between execution and deterrence—the idea that a potential murderer might not act because he feared execution. The study concluded that for every execution that occurred in the United States in the period 1933–1967, between seven and eight potential murders were avoided. Ehrlich's study was cited by then solicitor general Robert H. Bork in a speech to the Senate, and attracted a great deal of interest and serious debate.

A Matter of Common Sense
Ehrlich's work offers a scientific approach to something I've believed for years—namely, that executions can keep more murders from occurring. Even without the data, however, it's just a matter of common sense.

The death penalty is scary. No matter what method of execution is used, it sounds dreadful. Death is final, irrevocable. People fear it; therefore, if *anything* can keep one citizen from committing murder, it is the fear that he, too, will die. Penalties of any sort keep us in line—that's why our criminal justice system exacts them. And the stiffer the fine, the more severe the penalty, the greater the fear. It is this fear that keeps us in check.

Because the death penalty is the highest penalty, it would obviously evoke the most fear in a person. As legal expert Ernest van den Haag explains:

> The threat of 50 lashes deters more than the threat of 5: a $1000 fine deters more than a $10 fine; 10 years in prison deters more than 1 year in prison— just as, conversely, the promise of a $1000 reward is greater than the promise of a $10 reward, etc.[1]

It is true, of course, that most murders are not committed by rational, clear-thinking people. Most murders happen in the passion of the moment, and nobody with any sense is suggesting that these murderers are going to stop and weigh the consequences of what they are doing. On the other hand, serial killers, burglars, gang members, and others who plan their crime in advance can and do think of the possibilities. Many criminals forgo carrying weapons, for example, to keep from killing, as Senator Arlen Specter of Pennsylvania recalls:

> My twelve years' experience in the Philadelphia District Attorney's Office convinced me that the death penalty is a deterrent to crime. I saw many cases where professional burglars and robbers refused to carry weapons, for fear that a killing would occur and they would be charged with murder in the first degree, carrying the death penalty.[2]

No Such Thing as Life Without Parole

Many who want to be rid of the death penalty suggest that any stern punishment that is consistently and speedily exacted can be a deterrent to crime; therefore, they suggest, why not just sentence our most wicked criminals to life in prison without parole? We would no longer have to worry about them committing further crimes, plus society would not have to face the moral quandaries that occur when it kills a killer.

While I agree wholeheartedly that the best penalties are those that are fair and swift, I am always appalled that people can call for something as mythical as the sentence of life without possibility of parole. I don't believe there is such a thing. How do we know that such a prisoner can't escape or that later laws or court rulings could enable him to be paroled. That very thing happened in 1972, when the Supreme Court temporarily halted the death penalty after the *Furman vs. Georgia* decision.

All death row inmates had their sentences commuted, or changed, to life imprisonment. Most were released into the general prison population, often with frightening results. In Texas, for example, twelve of forty-seven commuted prisoners were responsible for twenty-one serious violent crimes against other inmates and staff. One killed another prisoner. One was released on parole (a new court ruling made that possible) and killed a young girl. Remember, these were criminals who had been supposedly sentenced to life in prison without parole.

And this brings up another troubling shortcoming of the life imprisonment sentence—what about prisoners who murder while in prison? For an inmate already serving a life sentence, how can you possibly deter him from further crimes unless there is something worse to fear?

"It Is, by God, a Specific Deterrent"

There is another aspect of the deterrence theory that is not, in my opinion, given enough credence, namely that no matter how abolitionists scoff at research like Ehrlich's, or at common sense, there is one thing that cannot be denied: The death penalty will always deter those who are executed. Obvious? Of course. But just because it is obvious, it is no less important or true, as death penalty advocate Thomas Sowell explains:

It is certainly not less important to the families of people murdered by those who have murdered before and who have been turned loose by judges or parole boards, or allowed weekend furloughs by "progressive" prison authorities. Whether these additional murders meet the statisticians' definitions of "significance," they are very significant to widows, orphans, and the parents of murdered children.[3]

Serial killer expert John Douglas, who has worked for twenty-five years with the FBI, agrees, and maintains that deterring that one criminal is reason enough to keep the death penalty as an option:

[The death penalty] is, by God, a specific deterrent. No one who has been executed has ever taken another innocent life. And until such time as we really mean it as a society when we say "imprisonment for life," I, and the families of countless victims, would sleep better at night knowing there is no chance that the worst of these killers will ever again be able to prey on others.[4]

Whether the death penalty deters that one specific criminal or a host of others doesn't matter. What matters is that innocent life will be spared—and that is reason enough to keep the death penalty.

1. Ernest van den Haag and John P. Conrad, *The Death Penalty: A Debate*. New York: Plenum Press, 1983, p. 69.

2. Arlen Specter, "Congress Must Make Death Sentences Meaningful Again," *Human Events*, July 15, 1994, p. 16.

3. Thomas Sowell, "Defenders of Murderers Spring into Action," *Manchester Union-Leader*, December 13, 1994, p. 21.

4. John Douglas and Mark Olshaker, *Journey into Darkness*. New York: Scribner, 1997, p. 169.

"The dim prospect of a possible death sentence and execution somewhere at the end of a fifteen-year procedural morass . . . isn't much of a deterrent."

The Death Penalty Is Too Inefficient to Deter Murder

One of the basic tenets of parenthood has to do with effective discipline: The closer the punishment is to the crime, the more effective it will be. In other words, the old notion of the harried mother threatening her misbehaving youngster with, "You just wait until your father gets home," is way off the mark, especially if she wants to teach her other children a lesson, too. By dinnertime when Dad gets home, the moment has passed, and any deterrence factor that might have existed when the crime occurred is long gone.

A Slowly Cranking Machine

The deterrence factor of the death penalty operates in much the same way. If we could punish murderers swiftly, in a matter of a few weeks, even hard-core abolitionists admit that we would see a marked decrease in the numbers of such crimes. Would-be murderers would stop and consider their acts if they knew justice would be swift and sure.

Swift justice is not a new concept; in fact, it's more common the further back in history one goes. Consider, for

48

instance, the case of Giuseppe Zangara, a mentally ill brick-layer who, on February 15, 1933, pulled a gun on President Franklin Roosevelt and fired repeatedly. Although Roosevelt was not harmed, Zangara killed Chicago mayor Anton J. Cermak. According to one modern writer, "Thirty-three days later—after arrest, guilty plea and sentence—Zangara was electrocuted in Florida's 'Old Sparky.' In the good old days of capital punishment, there wasn't even enough time to sign a book deal."[1]

Not these days. The machinery of justice—especially as it pertains to the death penalty—cranks very slowly. A person convicted today and sentenced to death waits an average of nine years until the date of execution; lots of prisoners wait longer. Gary Alvord, a triple murderer in Florida, has been waiting twenty-two years; one-fourth of the death row prisoners in Georgia have been there at least since 1980.

The reason for the long delays is built into the criminal justice system. Capital punishment statutes provide for an automatic review of every death sentence by a state appeals court. If that court upholds the death sentence, there are provisions for postconviction hearings in the state court system. And if there are any questions of federal law involved in the proceedings, the case can travel up to the Supreme Court. And all of this takes time—lots of it.

Though in recent months there have been attempts to speed the process along, little has changed. "State prosecutors' offices remain understaffed and overwhelmed," one writer reports, "courts have hopelessly long backlogs (assuming they can find lawyers for the defendants in the first place) and juries in most states enthusiastically continue to send killers to death row."[2]

Hardly a Deterrent

Today approximately three thousand people wait on death row in various prisons throughout the United States. For every person currently executed, five more are sentenced to be

executed. Experts say that just to meet this pace, we'd be executing one a day, 365 days a year, through the year 2021.

But there's not much chance of that happening, so the idea
of the death penalty as a deterrent doesn't seem to carry much
punch. As former FBI investigator John Douglas explains:

> If you're a young urban criminal making your living
> off the drug trade where there are huge amounts of
> money at stake and your business competition is out
> there trying to kill you every day, the dim prospect
> of a possible death sentence and execution some-
> where at the end of a fifteen-year procedural
> morass—that is, if you get caught, if you don't plea
> bargain, if you draw a tough judge and a tough jury,
> if you don't get reversed, if they don't change the
> law, et cetera, et cetera—isn't much of a deterrent,
> or a risk, for that matter, compared to the occupa-
> tional hazards you face on the street every day of
> your working life.[3]

How *can* prisoners fear execution when the leading cause of
death among death row prisoners is not lethal injection, electrocution, hanging, or poison gas, but natural causes?

Money Well Spent?

The long paper trails involved in trying and appealing (and
trying and appealing again and again) are not only time-
consuming, but costly. For example, California spends $90
million each year—that's taxpayer dollars—on capital cases. In
North Carolina each execution runs $2.6 million; each one in
Texas is about $2.3 million. Florida leads them all, with a sin-
gle execution costing taxpayers a whopping $3.2 million.

Surely the money could be better spent. A Duke University
study estimates that the fifty-six executions that occurred in
1995 cost Americans $121 million, enough to hire three thou-
sand police officers at $40,000 each.

The waste of time and money is irritating to everyone.
Federal judge Alex Kozinski complains:

We have constructed a machine that is extremely expensive, chokes our legal institutions, visits repeated trauma on victims' families and ultimately produces nothing like the benefits we would expect from an effective system of capital punishment.[4]

The New York State Bar Association agreed when in 1990 it concluded that the death penalty should go, in its words, because of "the enormous cost associated with such a measure, and the serious negative impact on the delivery of prosecution and defense services to the communities throughout the state that will result."[5]

There have been attempts to cut out the waste of money and time, but it's easier said than done. No judge wants to be accused of depriving a prisoner of an appeal or jeopardizing a conviction.

But enough is enough, said Arizona's Attorney General Grant Woods recently. He was so fed up with slow federal judges in his state that he did something drastic—he asked the U.S. federal court of appeals in San Francisco to order the Arizona judges to hurry up and make their rulings. The California court refused, and Woods is probably going to be waiting for his rulings in Arizona even longer, as one observer noted. "Trying to move a federal judge is like trying to make a pig dance," he said. "It doesn't work and it annoys the pig."[6]

Since it looks as though there won't be pigs dancing soon, the costly legal quagmire of death penalty litigation will almost guarantee that no criminals are going to be deterred from murder and mayhem anytime soon.

1. David A. Kaplan, "Anger and Ambivalence," *Newsweek*, August 7, 1995, p. 25.

2. Kaplan, "Anger and Ambivalence," p. 25.

3. John Douglas and Mark Olshaker, *Journey into Darkness*. New York: Scribner, 1997, p. 368.

4. Quoted in Kaplan, "Anger and Ambivalence," p. 25.

5. Quoted in Kaplan, "Anger and Ambivalence," p. 28.

6. Quoted in Kaplan, "Anger and Ambivalence," p. 28.

"Rather than deter homicide, executions have correlations to increases in the murder rate."

Improving Its Efficiency Will Not Make the Death Penalty a Deterrent

The idea of deterrence, the notion that the threat of execution for a crime frightens off a potential murderer, is a noble one. Of all the arguments used by those who favor the death penalty, it is the only one that seems humanitarian at its core. After all, it's not easy to argue for the death penalty based on vengeance or retribution; on the other hand, protecting innocent future victims by doing away with a few cold-blooded killers seems plausible, even to an opponent of the death penalty.

But as noble as it may sound, the idea of deterrence is only that—an idea. Nothing exists today that proves that putting prisoners to death keeps others from murder. Even if we were to speed up the process—greasing the wheels of the criminal justice system—there would be no deterrence. It just plain won't work.

Certainty of Punishment

Advocates of deterrence claim that the threat of being put to death for committing murder can strike fear into a potential murderer's heart. The very severity of the punishment—the electric chair, hanging, lethal injection—can do what life behind prison bars cannot do, they say.

But it's not the severity of the punishment that deters. If it were, wouldn't we still be boiling people in oil, or lopping off the hands of thieves, or chopping their heads off? Wouldn't we want the most severe punishment to be even more severe? And wouldn't we expect to see real results? And we'd do it in the public square at noon, and set up bleachers to make sure that everyone has a bird's-eye view, or televise it to the widest possible audience.

We've done that. That was how things used to be. But it didn't work; even though the punishments were gruesome and highly publicized, crime continued. Stories abound of pickpockets roaming the crowd, snatching purses of spectators who'd come to watch other pickpockets be executed. And one very busy operator of a guillotine in French Guiana named Hospel should have known better than most how grisly death by that machine was. But he himself committed murder, and was beheaded! If severity of punishment didn't deter Hospel, whom *could* it deter?

We have strived over the years to make executions less painful and bloody. The last public execution in this country took place in 1936. It is done now in the most private of ceremonies, where only a handful of people witness it. So how much deterrence could executions have now that they didn't have back in the days of public lynchings or beheadings?

No, I agree with a judge from Arkansas, Charles Isaac Parker, who said:

> It is not the severity of the punishment, but the certainty of it that checks crime nowadays. The criminal always figures on the chance of escape, and if you take that away entirely he stops being a criminal. The old adage of the law, "Certainty of punishment brings security" is as true today as it ever was.[1]

And is today, more than a century later.

"Murderers Are Not Like Most People"

Why then does the myth of deterrence continue? Why do some of us believe that executions deter people from committing murder? The answer, I think, is because we ourselves would be deterred. We would fear being caught and tried, we would fear being convicted and placed on death row. And we would fear death by gas, by lethal injection, by the electric chair. And that is the weakness of the deterrence theory—that we are *not* murderers, as researchers Donald Hook and Lothar Kahn write:

> Murderers are not like most people, except in that they are human. Murdering—killing—is deviant behavior, improbable behavior, unpredictable behavior. It is not likely, therefore, that before committing a crime, a murderer has nightmares about the prospect of a murder trial, a conviction, and death by whatever means. It may not even enter his consciousness.[2]

The Rev. Jesse Jackson agrees that the premise of deterrence gives a homicidal person far more credit for being rational than he or she deserves:

> If murderers were rational people educated in the laws of the states in which they live, the theory might have some weight. For criminals to be deterred by the [death] penalty, they both must know the possible penalties in the state where they commit their crimes and must rationally weigh the risks and benefits of their actions.[3]

Advocates of the death penalty turn to the social scientists to give weight to their position. University of Chicago economist Isaac Ehrlich, for example, maintained (in a flawed study) that for every murderer executed, seven or eight homicides were deterred.

Almost every modern social scientist scoffs at Ehrlich's methods today, and no one has been able to replicate his results. New studies have been done, and none supports the pro–death penalty folks. Some studies, in fact, show quite the opposite—that rather than deter homicide, executions have correlations to increases in the murder rate. In 1980 social scientists William Bowers and Glenn Pierce painstakingly analyzed the homicide records for New York State between 1907 and 1963 and found that in the months following every execution, there was an average increase of two or three murders. Known today as the "brutalization theory," the notion has gained wide acceptance.

Other research damns the deterrence supporters. A comparison of the murder rates in states with the death penalty and those without yields surprising results. Some studies, like that of University of Pennsylvania scholar Thorsten Sellen, found that in clusters of states matched along ethnic, religious, and economic lines, "the death penalty had no effect on the murder rates in the states examined."[4]

It gets worse for the execution advocates. Some recent studies even find that death penalty states have a *higher* murder rate. "If capital punishment saved lives," write researchers Ian Gray and Moira Stanley, "you would have less chance of being murdered in Florida, where the executioner is a friend, than in Michigan, which deported the executioner in 1847. However, the reverse is true."[5]

No, since neither common sense nor statistics can make a case for deterrence, the advocates of the death penalty ought to be honest with themselves. If executions appeal to them, defend them on the basis of something other than saving innocent lives. Vengeance, maybe.

1. Quoted in Frederick Drimmer, *Until You Are Dead: The Book of Executions in America.* New York: Citadel, 1990, p. 170.

2. Donald D. Hook and Lothar Kahn, *Death in the Balance: The Debate over Capital Punishment.* Lexington, MA: Lexington Books, 1989, p. 42.

3. Jesse Jackson, *Legal Lynching: Racism, Injustice, and the Death Penalty.* New York: Marlowe, 1996, p. 113.

4. Hook and Kahn, *Death in the Balance*, p. 45.

5. Ian Gray and Moira Stanley, eds., *A Punishment in Search of a Crime: Americans Speak Out Against the Death Penalty.* New York: Avon, 1989, p. 15.

CHAPTER 3

Is the Death Penalty Applied Unfairly?

"In eighty-two percent of [GAO] studies, race of the victim was found to influence the likelihood of being charged with capital murder or receiving the death penalty."

The Death Penalty Unfairly Targets Minorities

It's been the same story since our country was founded. There is one system of justice for the white majority. And there is another, hazy system that applies to people of color. Look back to the days of slavery. A white man who killed his black slave was guilty of no more than bad judgment, like a man who bought a dog that turned out to be mean. There was no trial, no punishment. But the slave who turned on his master? Put to death, hanged from the nearest stout branch.

Hard Times in Scottsboro

Now fast-forward to 1931, to Scottsboro, Alabama. Two white women accused nine young black men of rape. Although the men all denied the charges, they were convicted and all but one were sentenced to die in the electric chair.

Word of the case—along with the news that the "Scottsboro Boys," as they were known, had not had legal counsel—spread beyond the Deep South to the rest of the United States and Europe. People seemed surprised (they shouldn't have been) that such goings-on were tolerated, and demanded that the case be retried.

Eventually, public pressure convinced the U.S. Supreme Court to hear the case, and the nine justices decided that there were indeed grounds for a new trial. During the retrial, one of the plaintiffs admitted she had lied, and the young men were released. Although free, the men had suffered untold anguish and loss of reputation. The nearly two years they had spent in prison had left a huge gap in their young lives.

The story of the Scottsboro Boys is often cited to show that things have changed for the better. We've got lots of laws prohibiting discrimination that weren't on the books back in 1931, after all. And black Americans are no longer railroaded into guilty verdicts and inappropriately sentenced to death, right?

A white man smiles as a black man is prepared for execution.

Systemwide Discrimination

But racism is a devious thing. It can thrive regardless of laws and rules; it cannot be legislated away, no matter how hard we try. And as in education, in hiring, and in housing, racism continues to flourish in all aspects of the criminal justice system, including death sentencing.

Discrimination and the death penalty was addressed in the 1972 Supreme Court decision in *Furman vs. Georgia*, in which the death penalty, as it then was used, was declared unconstitutional and suspended. Before the *Furman* ruling, judges and juries were allowed wide discretion in imposing the death penalty or lesser sentences in murder cases. A great deal of inconsistency arose, as Jesse Jackson explains, "because of prejudice or sheer whim."[1]

The justices of the Supreme Court, in a 5-4 ruling, decided that the death penalty was indeed being applied in arbitrary, inconsistent ways, clearly a situation in which racism could prevail unchecked. The Court determined that until states eliminated this arbitrariness, prisoners could not be executed. Of course, those states that greatly favored the death penalty scrambled to rewrite their capital punishment laws to include various safeguards.

In time, these laws passed the inspection of the Court, so the death penalty could once more be used. Today, two-thirds of the states have death penalty statutes. But that certainly does not mean that racism has been *Furman*-ed out of the application of the death penalty—or any other aspect of our criminal justice system.

Shameful Statistics

For instance, when Joseph Green Brown (a fourteen-year veteran of death row whose conviction was reversed just hours before his execution) was asked about racism in his 1974 trial—after the *Furman* decision—he shook his head. "If you'd been at my trial in Florida," he said, "you'd have thought you were at a KKK [Ku Klux Klan] meeting and I was the guest of honor. I was the only black person in the whole court room."[2]

Death penalty opponents charge that changes made in the statutes were cosmetic only, that there is still far too much power in the hands of judges and juries who consistently misuse it. The statistics speak for themselves, and they are shameful. Today blacks make up 12 percent of our population, but account for 42 percent of the inmates on death row.

A look at individual states tells the same story—and northern states fare no better than the Deep South. In Virginia blacks make up only 19 percent of the population, but 50 percent of death row inmates. In Illinois, where blacks make up 15 percent of the population, 60 percent of death row inmates are black. Of Maryland's death row inmates, 80 percent are black, even though the state is only 25 percent black.

Looking at Victims

Other statistics reveal the death penalty's racist application. Since the death penalty was reinstated in 1976, eighty-one blacks have been executed for killing whites; only four whites have been executed for killing blacks. In the last two years, an amazing 95 percent of the victims of executed criminals were white.

Study after study has supported these findings, and eventually the evidence became so overwhelming that the federal General Accounting Office (GAO) did its own research. In a 1990 report, the GAO reviewed twenty-eight relevant studies and concluded:

> In eighty-two percent of the studies, race of the victim was found to influence the likelihood of being charged with capital murder or receiving the death penalty, i.e., those who murdered whites were found more likely to be sentenced to death than those who murdered blacks.[3]

Clearly, racism is still a cornerstone of the system. Even the Supreme Court, which in 1976 allowed the death penalty to squeak back in the legal door, is mindful of that fact. In 1987, eleven years after the death penalty was reinstated in Georgia, former justice William Brennan criticized the Court for continuing to uphold the death penalty: "[The] evidence shows that there is a better than even chance in Georgia that race will influence the decision to impose the death penalty: a majority of defendants in white victim crimes would not have been sentenced to die if their victims had been black."[4]

What the System Tells Us

Today in America, black Americans are eight times as likely to be a victim of murder than white Americans. Yet black Americans who murder white Americans are nineteen times as likely to be executed as white Americans who kill black Americans.

It's not difficult to see the message that's being communicated to Americans—some lives are valuable, others not. Maybe that message isn't overt, but, as Jackson claims, "Quietly and methodically, one prosecution at a time . . . our judicial system is demonstrably racist in the end result, and the end result—killing a disproportionate number of black males—matters."[5]

1. Jesse Jackson, *Legal Lynching: Racism, Injustice, and the Death Penalty*. New York: Marlowe, 1996, p. 44.

2. Quoted in George M. Anderson, "Fourteen Years on Death Row: An Interview with Joseph Green Brown," *America*, March 29, 1997, p. 18.

3. Quoted in Jackson, *Legal Lynching*, p. 103.

4. Quoted in Michael Ross, "Is the Death Penalty Racist?" *Human Rights*, Summer 1994, p. 25.

5. Jackson, *Legal Lynching*, pp. 104–105.

"We need to reject the notion . . . [that the death penalty is] a discriminatory tool against black Americans."

The Death Penalty Does Not Unfairly Target Minorities

There has been a great deal written over the years about the so-called discrepancies in the way Americans of color, especially black Americans, are sentenced in murder cases. In fact, one of the chief arguments heard against the death penalty is that it is racist. And since it is flawed in such a way, the argument goes, executions should be abolished.

That Was Then, This Is Now

The argument goes back to 1972, when the Supreme Court noted that racial discrimination had resulted in different patterns of sentencing and rates of execution for white convicted murderers and black convicted murderers. The Supreme Court's decision in *Furman vs. Georgia* was backed up by many studies that showed that blacks were executed at a rate far out of proportion to their numbers, and the Court urged states to rework their statutes to correct what it saw to be arbitrary and discriminatory use of the death penalty.

No one can doubt that in the past, racist attitudes accounted for inequity in many areas of social and political life in the United States. However, we need to reject the notion held by some that such attitudes persist today in making the death penalty a discriminatory tool against black Americans.

This is not to say, of course, that racism does not exist today; society is far from perfect. As long as ignorance exists in the world, it seems likely that there will always be some who prejudge on the basis of race. But that is certainly not the norm, as death penalty researchers Donald Hook and Lothar Kahn point out:

> The lot of the black murder suspect has improved in recent years. All-white juries in murder cases involving blacks have become rare. Prejudice may still exist in the jury room. . . . But the majority of Americans attempt to meet the challenge of fairness when put to the test.[1]

To eliminate the death penalty on the grounds that it *could conceivably* be racially biased is illogical. After all, the entire criminal justice system has the potential of discriminating on the basis of race (as almost anything in our society has) yet no one proposes dismantling that system. Using that logic, write social scientists Stanley Rothman and Stephen Powers, "would require us to condemn virtually every legal system in the history of the world."[2]

A Second Look at Those Numbers

Exactly what are abolitionists talking about when they refer to the "racist and discriminatory" use of the death penalty? Really, their argument is based on statistics, all of which are very misleading. For instance, they claim that based on percentages of murderers, more blacks are executed than whites. Even more compelling, blacks who kill whites are far more likely to get the death penalty than blacks who kill blacks.

Such a split-second analysis of statistics can't possibly yield any meaningful conclusions, however. Responsible social scientists have shown that by taking into account other significant factors, the relationship between a murderer's race and the chance of his getting executed evaporates.

Who Is Killing Whom?

One important study in 1987 shed some much needed light on the reasons for the discrepancy. For one thing, it found that the kinds of homicide committed by blacks tended to be those for which the death penalty is called for. Black-on-white murders (blacks as murderers, whites as victims) more frequently involved kidnapping and rape, mutilations, execution-style murders, tortures, and beatings. The murder of a police officer, another crime likely to qualify for the death penalty, tended to involve white victims, too—85 percent of police officers killed in the line of duty are white.

On the other hand, most homicides involving black victims stemmed from disputes or fights—homicides for which prosecutors rarely seek the death penalty. And it is important to remember that most of these murders were committed by blacks, not whites.

Seeing these statistics for what they really are is unsettling to the abolitionists. It tends to produce anger, especially among the white liberals, who would like to demonize the death penalty system. What is ironic, however, is that by proposing capital punishment's demise they are themselves devaluing the lives of the people they are trying to protect.

"A Cruel Victory, Indeed"

With the large numbers of murder victims who are black, and whose killers are black, why are the abolitionists fighting against a death penalty that will punish these killers? Why are they reluctant to support a system that will send the message that enemies of the black community will be punished in the extreme? As one expert writes:

> It would be a cruel victory, indeed, if, having struggled so long and so hard, and, finally, so successfully against all the forms of injustice imposed on them by the white population, they were now to be exposed to what may be—in part, at least—preventable black

crime because of the reluctance of white liberals to allow black criminals to be punished as they deserve to be punished. . . . A country that does not punish severely its black murderers thereby indicates that it does not regard murder to be a grave offense when it is committed in the black community.[3]

Ignore the numbers, I say. Whether the next ten death row inmates to be executed are black or white makes no difference. The only important question we must ask of each execution is: Was the person guilty? If the answer is yes, how could our system be flawed?

The fact that more blacks than whites might be caught or convicted is immaterial. If they are guilty, they must be punished, must they not? The fact (or perceived fact) that some deserving white criminals were *not* caught or convicted may point to trouble in the other aspects of the criminal justice system, but it says nothing about the death penalty.

"The guilty do not become innocent or less deserving of punishment because others escaped it," explains law expert Ernest van den Haag. "Justice remains just, however unequal, while injustice remains unjust, however equal."[4] That must be as true in the black community as in the white, no matter what the watchdogs of discrimination would have us believe.

1. Donald D. Hook and Lothar Kahn, *Death in the Balance: The Debate over Capital Punishment*. Lexington, MA: Lexington Books, 1989, p. 72.

2. Stanley Rothman and Stephen Powers, "Execution by Quota?" *Public Interest*, Summer 1994, pp. 12–13.

3. Walter Berns, *For Capital Punishment: Crime and the Morality of the Death Penalty*. New York: Basic Books, 1979, pp. 186–87.

4. Ernest van den Haag and John P. Conrad, *The Death Penalty: A Debate*. New York: Plenum Press, 1983, p. 225.

"Between 1900 and 1985, . . . 23 [people determined later to be innocent] were actually executed."

Innocent People Have Been Executed

In 1986 a young white woman was shot and killed at a dry cleaners in Monroeville, Alabama. The town was shocked by the murder; however, for the next eight months the police were unable to come up with any likely suspects. Finally, police arrested Walter McMillian, a black man who lived in a nearby town. Sources said he was not popular with many whites, for his son had married a white woman, and he himself was dating a white woman.

McMillian vehemently denied murdering the woman at the dry cleaners; he claimed he was at a fish fry all that day with relatives and friends. In fact, his story was corroborated by several people. Nevertheless, McMillian was arrested, tried, convicted, and imprisoned on death row even before formal sentencing.

McMillian was sentenced to death, writes one source, although "no physical evidence linked him to the crime, but three people testifying at his trial connected him with the murder. All three witnesses received favors from the state for their incriminating testimony."[1] Later, however, all three "witnesses" recanted their testimony; one stated that he had been pressured by the prosecutors to say that McMillian had been at the scene.

"Every Minute of Every Day, I Knew I Was Innocent"

For more than six years, Walter McMillian lived on death row while various appeals were filed in his behalf, all of which were denied. Eventually, however, new attorneys took over the case on a volunteer basis, and were able to demonstrate serious improprieties in the prosecution's case, such as withholding evidence that would have proved McMillian's innocence.

The television show *60 Minutes* featured McMillian's case in November 1992. Partly because of outraged public response to the report, Alabama agreed to begin a new investigation, and eventually admitted that a terrible mistake had been made. On March 3, 1993, McMillian was freed. In a Senate subcommittee hearing held later that year, he described his ordeal:

> I was wrenched from my family, from my children, from my grandchildren, from my friends, from my work that I loved, and was placed in an isolation cell, the size of a shoe box, with no sunlight, no companionship, and no work for nearly six years. Every minute of every day, I knew I was innocent.[2]

Not an Isolated Case

Walter McMillian's case, though tragic, could have had a far worse ending. He survived, although he was robbed of six years of his life, his honor and good name, his time with his grandchildren, and his work. As frightening as this case is, it's important to realize that this is not a one-in-a-million case. The history of the criminal justice system in America as elsewhere is rife with accounts of people who have been wrongly accused of heinous crimes and sentenced to death.

This is one of the most compelling reasons I can think of to get rid of the death penalty once and for all. If society executes an innocent person, there is no way the wrong can be righted. The penalty is irreversible, as too many innocent prisoners have already learned.

How many? In 1987 professors Michael L. Radelet and Hugo A. Bedau, two strong opponents of the death penalty, published a sensational research study in the *Stanford Law Review*. Their study, an in-depth look at death sentences handed down in the twentieth century, found that between 1900 and 1985, 349 people incorrectly convicted of capital crimes were later found to be innocent on the basis of the authors' reexamination of cases. Of these, 23 were actually executed.

Since 1970, there have been sixty-three prisoners released from death row around the United States, because evidence surfaced that proved them innocent. How much proof do we as a society need before we can accept the fact that our criminal justice system makes mistakes—life-and-death mistakes?

The Ways Things Go Wrong

"The fact that mistakes [in the system] are made," says Sister Helen Prejean, the author of *Dead Man Walking*, "will not surprise anyone with even cursory knowledge of the criminal justice system. It has been a sobering discovery for me to see just how flawed and at times chaotic the system of justice is."[3]

The flaws and chaos are everywhere in the system, and can affect the outcome of a case in many different ways. In their research, Radelet and Bedau found several key areas in which the system "broke down," including deliberately falsified testimony from witnesses, negligence on the part of attorneys or law enforcement personnel, coerced confessions, racial bias, and community pressure for a quick conviction.

And though some manage to luck out by having a higher court hear their case and reverse their death sentences—as in the case of Walter McMillian—most do not. Their cases are not reviewed in the media and do not appear on national television programs.

Second-Rate Legal Help?

That is because prisoners on death row are poor. None can afford high-powered attorneys—or *any* attorney, for that matter. Most are represented by court-appointed counsel, as is the right of people who cannot afford a lawyer. Unfortunately, these are generally the most underpaid, overworked attorneys, and because of the high turnover in public defenders offices, the least experienced. Do we think these lawyers are going to be eager to assist a prisoner on death row through the various appeals processes, especially knowing that the average stay on death row before execution is more than nine years?

Experts say that even finding a lawyer who has the energy, time, and financial resources (it's very costly, filing those petitions) to negotiate the complex legal web of death penalty statutes can be difficult. And if you do find someone, say experts, you most likely aren't getting great counsel. Admits one experienced trial lawyer, "A system being held together on the backs of counsel having to beg and borrow is guaranteed to provide second-rate representation."[4]

And what if a prisoner is so lucky as to get a competent, experienced death penalty lawyer? Contrary to popular belief, the endless series of legal appeals that death penalty opponents criticize rarely involve a reconsideration of a prisoner's guilt or innocence. If that were true, perhaps we would find more innocent men and women on death row around the country! Instead, it is death penalty procedures that are reviewed—whether various petitions were filed in time, for instance.

The Fallibility of Human Judgment

Such nuts-and-bolts court hearings, while important to make sure the process is constitutional in every way, cannot help the convict who desperately wants to prove his innocence. Even if a new bit of evidence surfaces that would prove a prisoner did not commit murder, for example, he might very well be unable to get such a hearing in which to introduce it. In most states, there simply is no formal procedure by which a defendant could produce new evidence of innocence before his execution.

More than two hundred years ago, the marquis de Lafayette had deep reservations about the death penalty, then a far more common punishment than today. "I shall ask for the abolition of the punishment of death," he stated, "until I have the infallibility of human judgment presented to me."[5]

Our criminal justice system, so large and so fraught with the potential for human error, is not good enough to wager human lives—innocent human lives. The fallibility of human judgment is unavoidable in such a human system.

1. Quoted in Hugo Adam Bedau, ed., *The Death Penalty in America: Current Controversies.* New York: Oxford University Press, 1997, p. 351.

2. Quoted in Bedau, *The Death Penalty*, p. 351.

3. Helen Prejean, *Dead Man Walking.* New York: Vintage Books, 1993, p. 220.

4 Quoted in Jesse Jackson, *Legal Lynching: Racism, Injustice, and the Death Penalty.* New York: Marlowe, 1996, p. 135.

5. Quoted in Donald D. Hook and Lothar Kahn, *Death in the Balance: The Debate over Capital Punishment.* Lexington, MA: Lexington Books, 1989, pp. 91–92.

"[It is] false sentimentality to argue that the death penalty ought to be abolished because of the abstract possibility that an innocent person might be executed."

Execution of an Innocent Person Should Not Preclude the Use of the Death Penalty

When all of their other arguments are knocked aside by logic and reasoning, those who want to abolish the death penalty pull out the Fear Card—the Old Maid of the death penalty deck—the one that says, "What if they execute an innocent person?"

The concept is scary, even the staunchest death penalty supporters will admit. No one wants to see an innocent man or woman die for a crime that was committed by someone else. However, it seems important to look at this risk in a more careful way.

The Case of Joseph Green Brown

Take, for example, the case of Joseph Green Brown, convicted of murder in Florida in 1974. He'd continually maintained his innocence, but the state had a star witness whose testimony all but sealed Brown's fate. He was sentenced to die in the electric chair.

In 1981 a lawyer named Richard Blumenthal—an advocate of the death penalty, by the way—was shown a copy of the transcript of Brown's trial by the NAACP (National Association for the Advancement of Colored People) Legal Defense Fund. Blumenthal agreed to take on Brown's case without pay, for he saw a number of what he believed to be injustices in the way the case had been handled.

"There were very significant shortcomings in the operation of the system," Blumenthal recalled later, "due to the incompetence of counsel representing [Brown] and mistakes made by prosecutors, some of them very likely deliberate."[1]

Blumenthal's suspicions paid off. Less than fifteen hours before Brown's scheduled execution, a U.S. court of appeals reversed the conviction, deciding that the prosecutor in the case had knowingly allowed perjured testimony from the key witness. Brown was freed after having spent more than fourteen years on death row.

Now, while some abolitionists would cite this case as evidence showing the injustices and faults of our criminal justice system (especially the death penalty), I do the opposite. I prefer to think that Brown's case demonstrates that the system *does* work. It may be slow, and it may be late, and it may come through unusual channels, but justice does arrive.

Reading the Fine Print

I'd get an argument from abolitionists who use a much-publicized study by Hugo Bedau and Michael Radelet to support their position. The study, published in 1987, claimed that in 350 cases defendants convicted of capital crimes were later found to be innocent. Sounds shocking, until you read the fine print.

What you'll learn is that 350 people were not wrongly executed. Of those 350 cases, only 200 of the allegedly wrongful convictions involved first-degree murders for which the death penalty was actually an option. Of those 200, only 139 were actually sentenced to death. Of those 139, only 23 were actually executed.

And whether those 23 were innocent is a matter not of hard evidence, but of pure speculation on the part of the researchers. As Bedau and Radelet themselves admit, "In none of these cases . . . can we point to the implication of another person or to the confession of the true killer; much less to any official action admitting the execution of an innocent person."[2]

So what's the big news here? We're talking about twenty-three people out of the more than seven thousand executions during the twentieth century in the United States who *may or may not have been* innocent. Forget the fact, says one expert, that in each case where there was a record to review, "there are eyewitnesses, confessions, physical evidence, and circumstantial evidence in support of the defendant's guilt."[3]

A Highly Complex System

One would think, listening to Bedau, Radelet, and their supporters, that the criminal justice system in the United States is operated by a few sadistic judges who are merely processing suspects on an assembly line from arrest to the electric chair. It's important to remember that the system is designed to protect the constitutional rights of each prisoner, particularly as a convicted death penalty prisoner nears his or her execution date.

Alex Kozinski, a federal judge who is himself a defender of the death penalty, explains that swift justice is impossible to find when the death penalty is concerned:

> Swift justice is hard to come by, because the Supreme Court has constructed a highly complex— and mutually contradictory—series of conditions that must be satisfied before a death sentence may be carried out. On the one hand, there must be individual justice, no matter how heinous the crime. On the other hand, there must be consistent justice: dis-

cretion to impose the death penalty must be tightly circumscribed. But individual justice is inherently inconsistent—different juries reach different results in similar cases. And there are scores of other issues that arise in every criminal case but take on special significance when death is involved.[4]

And, as Kozinski reminds us, the legal activity speeds up considerably in the waning moments of a convict's appeals process—again, evidence of the "leave no stone unturned" mentality of the criminal justice system:

> Last minute stay petitions in death cases are not unusual. They're a reflex. Except in rare cases when the prisoner decides to give up his appeal rights, death cases are meticulously litigated, first in state court and then in federal court—often bouncing between the two systems several times—literally until the prisoner's dying breath.[5]

Weighing the Advantages

It is certainly possible that an innocent person *could* be executed in our criminal justice system; it is, after all, a system devised and run by human beings. It is also possible that an innocent person has already been put to death.

Such thoughts are sobering, and remind all who are a part of that system what an awesome responsibility they have. However, the possibility that the ultimate error could occur should not be a reason to abolish the penalty. Even Hugo Bedau, the staunch opponent of the death penalty, acknowledges that it is "false sentimentality to argue that the death penalty ought to be abolished because of the abstract possibility that an innocent person might be executed."[6]

The risk of executing an innocent person is part of the price we must pay for law and order in our society. Obviously, we must all be diligent that such an error does not occur. But certainly, it would not be wise to abolish a useful tool merely because an unfortunate accident might occur. After all, most things people do can cause death to innocent people. We drive cars, we work in factories, we participate in sporting events, all of which can result in the death of people, through absolutely no fault of their own. Yet for someone to suggest that sports, driving, or working in factories should be outlawed would be ludicrous.

Death penalty advocate Ernest van den Haag explains it this way:

> Our government employs trucks. They run over innocent bystanders more frequently than courts sentence innocents to death. We do not give up trucks because the benefits they produce outweigh the harm, including the death of innocents. Many human activities, even quite trivial ones, foreseeably cause wrongful deaths. Courts may cause fewer wrongful deaths than golf.[7]

I can understand abolitionists' reluctance to embrace the death penalty on grounds of morality, or for religious reasons. I can even understand the difficulty of squaring the "cruel and unusual" argument with executing criminals. But to do away with capital punishment on the grounds that an accident might or might not occur is not even worth another word of discussion.

1. Quoted in George M. Anderson, "Fourteen Years on Death Row: An Interview with Joseph Green Brown," *America*, March 29, 1997, p. 20.

2. Quoted in Stephen Markman, "Innocents on Death Row?" *National Review*, September 12, 1994, p. 73.

3. Quoted in Markman, "Innocents on Death Row?" p. 72.

4. Alex Kozinski, "Tinkering with Death," *New Yorker*, February 10, 1997, p. 52.

5. Kozinski, "Tinkering with Death," p. 49.

6. Quoted in Walter Berns, *For Capital Punishment: Crime and the Morality of the Death Penalty*. New York: Basic Books, 1979, p. 178.

7. Quoted in Hugo Adam Bedau, ed., *The Death Penalty in America: Current Controversies*. New York: Oxford University Press, 1997, p. 451.

APPENDIX A

Views of the Death Penalty

Document 1: The Death Penalty Through Doctors' Eyes

Many moral arguments are made by opponents of the death penalty. Medical doctors, sworn to preserve life, are nevertheless needed in the execution process. In the article "Is Capital Punishment Ever Ethical?" from the July/August 1995 Hastings Center Report, *Dr. Richard H. Nicholson addresses the issues with which many doctors struggle.*

This is not the place to rehearse the arguments against capital punishment, other than to recall that all methods in use, except lethal injection, are designed to cause pain as well as kill. Several electrocutions in recent years have taken more than fifteen minutes to kill the condemned man, and meanwhile he has been severely burnt. How can it serve the purposes of a modern society to condone such torture?

What is relevant to the interests of bioethicists, however, is the issue of the involvement of physicians in capital punishment. While lethal injections may be the least inhumane form of execution, they are also the form most likely to need the assistance of health care personnel acting in direct contravention of their duty to preserve life. The involvement of health care personnel in capital punishment, in any role other than certifying death, has been declared unethical by the World Medical Association, the World Psychiatric Association, the International Council of Nurses, and Amnesty International. Even if there is no longer any direct participation of doctors in U.S. executions, there appear to be several examples of direct involvement.

One of the most curious of these, to European eyes, is that psychiatrists who have not examined a convicted murderer may nevertheless testify to his continuing dangerousness, and thereby influence the imposition of the death sentence. Psychiatrists also face the appalling dilemma of whether to treat a mentally ill condemned man, knowing that untreated he cannot be executed, but that if treatment is successful he could be found to be "fit to be executed"—another concept Europeans find difficult to fathom.

Regardless of the unanimity of the international bodies mentioned above, some U.S. doctors are still involved in executions either by helping to find veins into which to put lethal injections, or by advising on whether prisoners are dead or need another dose of whatever substance—gas, electricity, poison, or bullet—is being used.

Document 2: The War of the Currents

In the 1880s, when knowledge about electricity was in its infancy, there was much talk about which type of current was most useful and safe—alternating current or

76

direct current (today's AC and DC). In his book Until You Are Dead: The Book of Executions in America, *Frederick Drimmer shows how two well-known inventors' varying ideas about electricity led to speculation about electrocution as a way of executing criminals.*

Thomas Alva Edison . . . had developed the first electric power system in 1882. Convinced the future belonged to his low tension direct current, he'd sunk a fortune into its development and promotion. Pitted against Edison was another industrial Goliath, George Westinghouse, Jr. Westinghouse current (as alternating current was often called) had some striking advantages: high voltages could be transmitted over great distances and at extremely low costs. Direct current, by contrast, could be sent only over short distances and at low voltages. It was distinctly the less economical of the two.

But direct current is much safer! cried Edison. Alternating current, with its powerful voltages, could easily produce a fatal shock. It was too dangerous for electric lights and other everyday purposes. By the same token, he suggested insidiously, it was superbly adapted for use in electrical executions. When anyone touched an exposed live wire powered by alternating current, he died as instantly as if he'd been struck by lightning. Westinghouse retorted that Edison was mistaken; alternating current was much safer than direct.

It was called "the war of the currents," and Edison fought to win it with every trick that he knew. He worked hard to persuade local legislators around the country to pass laws banning electric systems powered by alternating generators. As part of his campaign, he put on demonstrations at his Menlo Park laboratory in West Orange, New Jersey. He paid the children of the neighborhood twenty-five cents for each stray cat and dog they could bring him. Then the barking, mewing procession was forced onto a sheet of tin charged with a high voltage from an alternating generator and instantly executed. These demonstrations resulted in at least one of his employees receiving such a shock that forever after he had "the awful memory of body and soul being wrenched asunder."

Harold P. Brown, an electrical engineer, played a key role in persuading the New York State legislature to make electricity—and specifically the kind produced by a Westinghouse alternating generator—the official method of execution. Brown (it can hardly be a coincidence) had once worked for Edison. He traveled up and down the state delivering public lectures in which he asserted that "with a pressure of 1,500 volts there cannot be the slightest doubt of instantaneous death." To show how instantaneous, Brown put animals to death in demonstrations reminiscent of Edison's. Infuriated, Westinghouse waged a tireless campaign of counterpropaganda.

Document 3: More Barbaric than Before?

In his book Lords of the Scaffold: A History of the Executioner, *Geoffrey Abbott discusses the beginnings of the gas chamber as a means of executing crim-*

inals. Begun in 1924, it was hailed as a humane means of death, one that would replace the more barbaric forms of execution such as firing squad and hanging. As Abbott notes, however, the gas chamber received more criticism than praise.

As its name implies, the gas chamber is a small airtight room made of steel, with a plate glass observation window, containing one or more chairs bolted to the floor. The victim is strapped into a chair, near to which is positioned a container of sulphuric acid.

After the room has been vacated by the officials and the signal given, the executioner in the adjoining control room pulls a red-painted lever. This turns a rod extending into the gas chamber, alllowing it to lower a cloth sachet of sodium cyanide pellets into the acid. The chemical reaction so generated gives off hydrogen cyanide (HCN), prussic acid.

Exposure to 300 parts of this lethal cocktail per one million parts of air is rapidly fatal, almost instantaneous death from asphyxiation resulting, if the victim breathes deeply. As with most "instantaneous" methods of execution, it does not always pay to believe the advertisements.

In the same way as the electric chair became popular with some states, so others adopted the gas-chamber method, one being installed in San Quentin Prison, California. In the 1930s San Francisco newspapers, the *Examiner*, the *Chronicle*, and others devoted many paragraphs to this latest innovation, especially when the city authorities tested the apparatus on live pigs. Many of the reporters who attended, hoping for some good copy, were repelled by what they saw, some describing it as more savage than being hanged, drawn, and quartered.

Document 4: An Unconstitutional Penalty

The Furman vs. Georgia *case halted capital punishment in the United States between 1972 and 1976. The justices of the Supreme Court were not in agreement, however, on the reasons they found the death penalty unconstitutional. The following is an excerpt from Justice William O. Douglas's opinion, which is included in* Furman v. Georgia: The Constitution and the Death Penalty, *by Burt Henson and Ross Olney. Douglas feels that the death penalty was often discriminatory as applied to people of color and the poor.*

In a nation committed to equal protection of the laws there is no permissible "caste" aspect of law enforcement. Yet we know that the discretion of judges and juries in imposing the death penalty enables the penalty to be selectively applied, feeding prejudices against the accused if he is poor and despised, lacking political clout, or if he is a member of a suspect or unpopular minority, and saving those who by social position may be in a more protected position. . . . The high service rendered by the "cruel and unusual" punishment clause of the 8th amendment is to require legislatures to write penal laws that are even handed, non-selective, and non-arbitrary, and to require judges to see to it that general laws are not applied sparsely, selectively, and spottily to unpopular groups. . . .

Thus these discretionary statutes are unconstitutional in their operation. They are pregnant with discrimination and discrimination is an ingredient not compatible with the idea of equal protection of the laws that is implicit in the ban on "cruel and unusual" punishments.

Document 5: The High Price of Death

British writer Stephen Trombley, in his book The Execution Protocol: Inside America's Capital Punishment Industry, *spends time with a Boston inventor named Fred Leuchter, who invented the lethal injection machine and makes his living selling other execution hardware. In the following excerpt, Leuchter itemizes the costs for the equipment he sells.*

I asked Fred about the cost of his various execution systems. The cheapest is the modular lethal injection system at $30,000. His preferred method of execution, the electric chair, sells for $35,000. A gallows, because it is an unusual and infrequently requested product, sells for $85,000. The most expensive execution product is a Fred Leuchter gas chamber, costing more than $200,000. Fred had created another product designed for states which either have no execution facilities in their new prisons or have not carried out an execution for many years. The Leuchter "Execution Trailer" provides a mobile execution facility including a lethal injection machine, a steel holding cell for the inmate, and separate areas for the witnesses, chaplain, prison workers, and medical personnel, at a cost of $100,000.

Of all Fred's execution products, the electric chair presents the state with the cheapest consumables bill at the end of the day. Only thirty-one cents' worth of electricity is required to electrocute someone in the Leuchter chair. The chemicals for lethal injection cost between $600 and $700, while the cyanide required for a gas chamber execution costs around $250.

I was anxious to see how profitable Fred's business had been. He told me, "The state shouldn't be over a barrel to bring in somebody that's going to haul them over the coals and charge them a small fortune for executing somebody. Executions are not something people should be making money hand over fist on. I don't make any bones about it, I have a twenty percent markup on my equipment, and I think that's more than fair. And I think anybody that would try to price the equipment would come back and think I was making less. I have people who when they find out what my prices are, they say, 'That's all?'"

Document 6: "A Wretched Lot"

In his book Legal Lynching: Racism, Injustice, and the Death Penalty, *Jesse Jackson discusses why, in his opinion, deterrence is not a good argument for applying the death penalty.*

Deterrence depends on would-be murderers identifying with the executed killer. The problem with that logic is that countless psychological studies show that we identify with those whom we admire or envy.

Condemned prisoners who arrive at the electric chair are a wretched lot. Since they are generally loners and social outcasts who are uneducated and have committed brutal and cowardly crimes, it is highly unlikely that calculating killers would identify with them. The contrast they see between themselves and the condemned may actually lead prospective killers to determine that the death penalty is reserved for people unlike themselves.

The associations that do take place are a sort of "villain identification." The would-be murderer identifies the executed killer with someone who has gravely offended or threatened him, and thus sees himself in his crime as an executioner administering justice. The lesson the murderer takes from the execution is that killing someone whose actions you despise and abhor is not only acceptable but officially sanctioned.

As historical evidence, [researchers] Bowers and Pierce recalled a horrifying and shameful era in our nation's past—the lynching of black men by white mobs. Since 1890, nearly 3,500 lynchings have been documented, even though lynching a person was a capital crime in many of the states in which they occurred. (So much for deterrence.) The chillingly execution-like scene of an angry white mob leading a shackled "prisoner" to the noose certainly tells me that it wasn't the condemned prisoners the vicious mobs were identifying with during these "official" executions.

Document 7: A Different Sort of Job

What sort of person willingly assists the executioner? Joe Ferretti, a longtime member of the staff of the San Quentin gas chamber, describes his work in this excerpt from the essay "The Fraternity of Death" by Michael A. Kroll, contained in the book Facing the Death Penalty: Essays on a Cruel and Unusual Punishment, *edited by Michael L. Radelet.*

A short, affable man, Ferretti does not look like his 79 years. When it comes to the gas chamber, there are few people, living or dead, with as much experience as he has. In his 29 years at San Quentin, Ferretti participated in 126 executions. "I called my job baby-sitting," he says, "but the official name was death watch officer."

Ferretti was the officer at the main gate before he got into this other line of work. He liked working outdoors and meeting the public. He remembers wondering how anyone could work in the gas chamber—until he was asked to do the job. "First I went home and asked my wife," he says. "She said it was all right with her if it was all right with me. So I tried it." He remained at the job for the next 27 years. "I still kept my regular job at the front gate," he says, "but they'd assign someone else to do it when I was on death watch."

"We earned $15 for death duty in the beginning," he says, chuckling. "The last one I got $75. The executioner was making a lot more—$500, I think. He's dead now. Pretty near everyone's dead now."

Of his more recent experience as teacher to the new crop of executioners, he says, "I showed them the regular routine—what we done when I
was there. We did executions at ten in the morning on Friday. On
Thursday, around four, we'd go upstairs and get the inmate and bring him
downstairs to the death cell next to the gas chamber. Then we'd stay there,
two of us, till about 9:45 the next morning. We'd change his clothes to
fresh jeans and a white shirt without any pockets, and no underwear or
shoes. I guess gas could accumulate in places like that, and when you went
in to get him you could get a whiff of the stuff."

After strapping the condemned man into the chamber and sealing the
great steel door of the tank, he waited. "When the doctor says he's dead,"
Ferretti continues, "we start the pumps to pump the gas into the air outside. In about fifteen minutes, we crack the door a bit and turn a valve that
lets air in the bottom. You have to pump for about half an hour before you
can get in. Then two of us go in with a garden sprayer filled with ammo-
nia to spray around his pants and clothes. It kind of neutralizes the gas. We
go in in a hurry and unbuckle the straps. One grabs one side and one the
other, and we scoot him into a redwood box made by prisoners in the car-
pentry shop. It's waiting just outside the door. Then a truck picks it up and
takes it to the prison hospital, where the family claims it."

Document 8: Singling Out Targets for the Death Penalty

In his article "The Powers Behind the Death Penalty" for the Witness, *Steven
Charleston explains why he thinks that the use of the death penalty signals the real
collapse of a community.*

Capital punishment . . . is the wrong debate about the right problem. The
issue is justice, but justice on a level far deeper than legal execution. The
irony is: The more we claim the death penalty as a legal means of deterrence to crime, the more we subvert the true debate over justice as a deterrence to community collapse. While the average citizen feels a growing
uneasiness about how things are going on the local level, the authorities
attempt to reassure the populace by calling for more firepower, for polic-
ing agencies and tougher penalties for an ever expanding list of criminals.
That list itself begins to single out certain target communities that are
identified as the source of social breakdown. Immigrants, political dissi-
dents, racial minorities: These are the usual suspects to be blamed when a
culture begins to fear itself. In response, citizens are asked to believe that
if only there were more police, more jails, and more executions, then the
tide would turn. Shifting public attention from the deeper justice issues to
the shallower formula of scapegoats and promises of restoring law and
order accomplishes two primary goals for the defenders of the status quo:
It distracts the focus of the public debate from the root causes of community dissolution and it justifies the expenditure of more and more resources
to preserve the power of those in charge.

Document 9: A New Lease on Life

In May 1963, Darryl Bell was charged with murder; he was found guilty and sentenced to death. Minutes before his execution, after having his head shaved for the electric chair, Bell was granted a stay of execution, and later his sentence was commuted, or reduced. Today he is a free man. Bell talks about being placed back in the general prison population from death row in this excerpt from A Punishment in Search of a Crime, *edited by Ian Gray and Moira Stanley.*

A lot of the inmates believe and expected us [death row inmates] to come out vegetables, because of the stress you go through. When we came out we began to go to school and get involved in the exercise, the football, the handball. I mean, we were just happy to be free, so that any energy we put forth was to us a new reality. They thought those guys are crazy out there in the cold weather playin' ball. But to me it was freedom. You know, not being handcuffed everywhere you go, I felt free. I just knew somehow that the Lord would allow me to come out of there. I just felt that some-how. . . .

When I was released from death row, the warden gave me the job of working with the camera in the visiting room. I took pictures, I was the photographer. That was just one of the jobs I did and that allowed me to become more in tune to people. You know, I was just not used to being around people, and when the people would come in, I was shy, you know. I would also be the babysitter when families would come in to visit the husbands. I made a lot of friends in Gradeford, so that when the men's children would come and they wanted to be with their wives and girl-friends and family, I would take the kids over to the side where the camera was, and that's how I started to feel at ease around people.

The kids really helped me. They made me laugh. I was afraid to laugh and to do this and to do that, but it worked its way out. I didn't have too many suspicions about people and I guess that was because I felt so happy to be free. I didn't have time to think about the other part.

Document 10: Getting What You Pay For

In her book Dead Man Walking, *Helen Prejean talks with lawyer Millard Farmer about the difficulty most death row inmates have in getting competent legal help—specifically in the case of young Pat Sonnier, a prisoner soon to be executed.*

Millard explains that he'll raise [in an appeals petition] the issue that Pat's attorney was ineffective, but he doesn't have much hope that the courts will agree with him. It's rare nowadays in capital cases, he says, for the courts to concede that defense attorneys are ineffective. "I mean, there are cases where defense attorneys in capital cases have actually shown up for trial drunk, or so ill prepared they told the judge they didn't know what they were doing, and even then the appeal courts wouldn't concur on the ineffectiveness of counsel." He points out that public defenders, especial-ly in Southern states, have so many clients to defend they can scarcely manage to interview them before trial, much less do the time-consuming investigation that capital cases require.

It's not a fluke, Millard says, that 99 percent of death-row inmates are poor. "They get the kind of defense they pay for." He explains that the high court's stringent standard of judging ineffectiveness of counsel now puts the burden of proof on a defendant's appellate attorney to demonstrate that defense counsel blunders directly affect the jury's verdict, and that minus those blunders the jury would have returned a different verdict. "But how are you going to demonstrate that, of all the variables in a case, a mistake of the defense counsel caused the jury to render a certain verdict? The court just comes back and says the attorney's mistakes were 'harmless error' and the jury would have returned a guilty verdict anyway. Every person is supposed to have a constitutional right to effective assistance of counsel, but the courts, by imposing such impossible procedural strictures have reamed out that right to an empty shell."

Pat's trial attorney failed him most of all during the sentencing part of the trial, Millard says. "That's when you want to try to get family, friends, employers, clergy, who know your client, to speak for him. If the jury can see your client as a human being, no matter what terrible crime he or she may have done, your client has a chance to live." In Pat's first trial, he says, other than the attorney, there was no one to speak for his life—only a photocopied report of a psychologist who wasn't even in the courtroom.

Document 11: A Judge's Distance

Although judges have an awesome responsibility in the sequence of appeals during the death penalty process, most know the defendants who appear in their courtrooms as faces only. In his article for the February 10, 1997, New Yorker, Judge Alex Kozinski ponders the fact that he has never witnessed the execution of any of the men he has sent to the electric chair.

Though I've now had a hand in a dozen or more executions, I have never witnessed one. The closest I came was a conversation with Bill Allen, a lawyer from my former law firm. I ran into him at a reception and his face was gray, his eyes—usually sharp and clear—seemed out of focus.

"Not well," Bill answered when I asked how he was doing. "I lost a client. His name was Linwood Briley. I saw him die in the electric chair a couple of days ago."

"Was it rough?"

"What do you think? It was awful."

"What was it like when they turned on the juice?"

"Oh, by the time they got done strapping him down, putting the goop on his head and the mask on his face, the thing sitting in that chair hardly looked human. But the really strange part was before: looking at him, talking to him, even joking with him, fully aware that he'd be dead in half an hour."

"Why did you go?"

"I thought he should have a friend there with him in his final minutes."

The look on Bill's face stayed with me a long time. It was enough to persuade me that I'd never want to witness an execution. Yet I sometimes wonder whether those of us who make life-and-death decisions on a regular basis should not be required to watch as the machinery of death grinds up a human being. I ponder what it says about me that I can, with cool precision, cast votes and write opinions that seal another human being's fate but lack the courage to witness the consequences of my actions.

Document 12: "The Only Way I Can Go On"

There is disagreement about whether Timothy McVeigh should be put to death, even among the families of those who died in the Oklahoma City bombing. In the following passage from "The Families Debate McVeigh's Fate," in the June 16, 1997, Newsweek, *Bud Welch explains why he is against the death penalty. Welch's daughter Julie was killed in the blast.*

Most people believe Timothy McVeigh should be put to death. I certainly understand their anger: my daughter Julie, a Spanish-language translator who worked for the Social Security Administration at the Murrah building, lost her life in the bombing. I am filled with rage at McVeigh. But I don't think he should be executed.

I'm not a minister or philosopher and I'm not an anti–death penalty crusader. But executing a murderer is just another kind of murder. When Julie was at Marquette University, we'd debate politics during the long drive between Oklahoma City and Milwaukee. One time she said something I've recalled a lot recently: "Dad, the death penalty doesn't teach us anything but hate."

McVeigh shouldn't get off easy. Lock him up for good, with no chance to get out. Is that punishment enough? The part of me that still screams "kill him" doesn't think so. But my Catholicism teaches that even he has a soul, and we must at least try to save him—and even try to forgive him. I'm still too angry to deal with that now. But I'll have to be forgiving if I am to have peace. That would be harder if he is executed. I don't want McVeigh's death on my head. A lady from Texas called me and said her husband had been murdered. After his killer was executed, she began to feel guilty. She thought knowing the murderer was dead would help ease her grief, but it didn't—and I don't think it would help me, either.

I am not trying to win converts. I just want people to think hard about the costs of the death penalty. Killing McVeigh won't bring my daughter back. The only way I can go on is to continue to believe in the sanctity of life—even a mass murderer's.

APPENDIX B

Facts About the Death Penalty

• Thirty-eight states presently allow the death penalty. Alaska, Hawaii, Maine, Michigan, Minnesota, Iowa, Wisconsin, Rhode Island, Vermont, Massachusetts, North Dakota, West Virginia, and the District of Columbia do not.

• By far the most common method of execution as of 1997 is lethal injection, followed by electrocution. Only seven states (Arizona, California, Maryland, Mississippi, Missouri, North Carolina, and Wyoming) execute criminals by lethal gas; three (Washington, Delaware, and New Hampshire) employ hanging. Firing squads are used in Idaho, Oklahoma, and Utah.

• Research shows that a death penalty case costs between $4 and $5 million from trial through execution.

• Of death row inmates in 1996, 48 percent are white, 41 percent are black, and 7 percent are Hispanic.

• As of 1997, there are 3,182 inmates awaiting execution in the United States.

• Lethal gas was introduced in 1924 in Nevada; the electric chair was first used in New York in 1890.

• The last public execution in the United States was that of Rainey Bethea in Owensboro, Kentucky. A crowd of twenty thousand gathered to watch the hanging.

• The abolitionist movement got a lift when Helen Prejean's book *Dead Man Walking* was made into an award-winning film in 1995. The film starred Susan Sarandon and Sean Penn; Sarandon received the Academy Award for Best Actress.

• Texas leads the nation in the number of executions since the death penalty's revival in 1976, with ninety-two.

• Texas and California lead the other states with four hundred convicts on death row.

• Most European countries have banned the death penalty; some countries that still use it are China, Iraq, Libya, Uganda, and Zaire—all nations known for their human rights violations.

• In 1996 no sitting Supreme Court justice believed the death penalty to be unconstitutional.

• Eighty-two percent of the murder victims in cases resulting in executions since 1976 have been white, even though whites are victims in less than half of the murders committed each year in the United States.

• In Kentucky as of 1997, every convict on death row is there for the murder of a white victim, despite the fact that there have been one thousand blacks murdered there since 1976.

• The pay for death penalty lawyers is very low—$1,000 for out-of-court work on cases that, if handled properly, take hundreds of hours of work.

• There has not been an execution in more than thirty years in the United Kingdom.

• Since the *Furman* decision, of the 4,702 inmates sentenced to death, only 188 have been executed.

• Opinion polls show that 60 percent of people questioned reject the death penalty when offered the alternative of life in prison without parole.

STUDY QUESTIONS

Chapter 1

1. According to the author of Viewpoint 1, how does the death penalty's history affect whether it is legally just or unjust today?

2. Does the author of Viewpoint 2 feel that injustice has been addressed adequately as it relates to the death penalty? Do you agree?

3. Explain the Marshall Hypothesis, as introduced in Viewpoint 3. Do you feel this is an accurate assessment of public sentiment today?

4. Why does the author of Viewpoint 4 think "humane" forms of execution are unnecessary? Should humaneness be a part of society's deliberations on executing criminals like John Albert Taylor? Why or why not?

Chapter 2

1. Do you think Douglas's argument in Viewpoint 1 about "specific deterrence" justifies capital punishment? Explain your answer.

2. Why does the author of Viewpoint 2 feel that deterrence is weakened when executions are expensive or when they are delayed?

3. Do you agree with Jesse Jackson's opinion in Viewpoint 3 that murderers are not rational? What would Jackson say about Ernest van den Haag's logic of "the 50 lashes" in Viewpoint 1?

Chapter 3

1. Is it fair to use the Scottsboro trial, introduced in Viewpoint 1, as evidence of racism in the United States? Why or why not?

2. According to Viewpoint 2, is racism a concern today in death penalty cases? Is it important to assess the race of murder victims as well as murderers? Why or why not?

3. Do you agree with Helen Prejean's statement in Viewpoint 3 that the American system of justice is flawed and chaotic? Give examples to support your answer.

4. In Viewpoint 4, why does Ernest van den Haag feel that an occasional mistake in death penalty cases is not a problem? Do you agree with him? What would Helen Prejean's response be?

FOR FURTHER READING

Amnesty International Publications, *United States of America: The Death Penalty*. London: Amnesty International, 1987. Excellent appendixes about death penalty procedures.

Hugo Adam Bedau, *Death Is Different: Studies in the Morality, Law, and Politics of Capital Punishment*. Boston: Northeastern University Press, 1987. Good section on the politics of the death penalty.

Stephen A. Flanders, *Capital Punishment*. New York: Facts On File, 1991. Very thorough annotated bibliography.

JoAnn Bren Guernsey, *Should We Have Capital Punishment?* Minneapolis: Lerner Publications, 1993. Very readable, good illustrations.

Burt Henson and Ross R. Olney, *Furman v. Georgia: The Constitution and the Death Penalty*. New York: Franklin Watts, 1996. Excellent quotations from Supreme Court justices.

Elaine Landau, *Teens and the Death Penalty*. Hillside, NJ: Enslow, 1992. Helpful introduction, easily understood.

David Lester, *The Death Penalty: Issues and Answers*. Springfield, IL: Charles C. Thomas, 1987. Good starting point for research.

Robert H. Loeb Jr., *Crime and Capital Punishment*. New York: Franklin Watts, 1986. Interesting reading; helpful information for younger readers trying to draw their own conclusions about the death penalty.

David von Drehle, *Among the Lowest of the Dead: The Culture of Death Row*. New York: Random House, 1995. Interesting information on the psychology of death row and the emotions and fears surrounding the death penalty.

WORKS CONSULTED

Books

Geoffrey Abbott, *Lords of the Scaffold: A History of the Executioner*. London: Robert Hale, 1991. Interesting information about punishment through history.

Hugo Adam Bedau, ed., *The Death Penalty in America: Current Controversies*. New York: Oxford University Press, 1997. Excellent bibliography and notes.

Walter Berns, *For Capital Punishment: Crime and the Morality of the Death Penalty*. New York: BasicBooks, 1979. Helpful information about the use of the death penalty around the world.

Donald A. Cabana, *Death at Midnight: The Confessions of an Executioner*. Boston: Northeastern University Press, 1996. Interesting behind-the-scenes information about prison administration.

John Douglas and Mark Olshaker, *Journey into Darkness*. New York: Scribner, 1997. Helpful final chapter on the need for the death penalty.

Frederick Drimmer, *Until You Are Dead: The Book of Executions in America*. New York: Citadel, 1990. Very readable; good section on people who narrowly escaped being wrongly executed.

Lawrence M. Friedman, *Crime and Punishment in American History*. New York: BasicBooks, 1993. Good section on the historical racism of the death penalty.

Ian Gray and Moira Stanley, eds., *A Punishment in Search of a Crime: Americans Speak Out Against the Death Penalty*. New York: Avon, 1989. Interesting array of essays; helpful bibliography.

David Freeman Hawke, *Benjamin Rush: Revolutionary Gadfly*. Indianapolis: Bobbs-Merrill, 1971. Excellent background on early anti–death penalty sentiment in America.

Donald D. Hook and Lothar Kahn, *Death in the Balance: The Debate over Capital Punishment*. Lexington, MA: Lexington Books, 1989. Very readable, good section on deterrence.

Jesse Jackson, *Legal Lynching: Racism, Injustice, and the Death Penalty*. New York: Marlowe, 1996. Highly readable; good sections on discrimination against the poor and black in death penalty cases.

Helen Prejean, *Dead Man Walking*. New York: Vintage Books,

1993. Very intense, excellent work from an abolitionist perspective.

Michael L. Radelet, ed., *Facing the Death Penalty: Essays on a Cruel and Unusual Punishment*. Philadelphia: Temple University Press, 1989. Somewhat difficult reading, but excellent material on the "cruel and unusual" arguments.

Mark Siegel, Carol Foster, and Nancy Jacobs, eds., *Capital Punishment*. Wylie, TX: Information Aids, 1988. Helpful quotations from Supreme Court briefs.

Gail B. Stewart, *Life During the Spanish Inquisition*. San Diego: Lucent Books, 1998. Helpful information on the use of torture as punishment.

Stephen Trombley, *The Execution Protocol: Inside America's Capital Punishment Industry*. New York: Crown, 1992. Good chapter on the man behind the electric chair; helpful notes.

Ernest van den Haag and John P. Conrad, *The Death Penalty: A Debate*. New York: Plenum Press, 1983. Helpful debate format; each author summarizes best arguments for and against capital punishment.

Periodicals

George M. Anderson, "Fourteen Years on Death Row: An Interview with Joseph Green Brown," *America*, March 29, 1997, p. 17.

————, "Opposing the Death Penalty: An Interview with Helen Prejean," *America*, November 9, 1996, p. 8.

Steven Charleston, "The Powers Behind the Death Penalty," *Witness*, September 1997, p. 12.

Alexander Cockburn, "Beat the Devil," *Nation*, June 26, 1995, p. 911.

Stuart A. Creque, "Killing with Kindness," *National Review*, September 11, 1995, p. 51.

Nick DiSpoldo, "Capital Punishment and the Poor," *America*, February 11, 1995, p. 8.

Jean Bethke Elshtain, "The Hard Questions," *New Republic*, June 16, 1997, p. 27.

"The Families Debate McVeigh's Fate," *Newsweek*, June 16, 1997, p. 30.

Don Feder, "Pity the Poor Killers, Execution Hurts," *Conservative*

Chronicle, February 14, 1996, p. 20.

Burk Foster and Craig J. Forsyth, "Meanest of All," *Angolite*, July/August 1994, p. 26.

Bruce Frankel and Fannie Weinstein, "Fighting for Life," *People*, August 19, 1997, p. 93.

Martin Garbus, "Executioner's Song," *Nation*, December 19, 1994, p. 746.

Joanne Gross, "Deliberations of Mortals and the Grace of God," *America*, November 9, 1996, p. 17.

Nat Hentoff, "Why Not Air Killings on TV?" *Liberal Opinion Week*, March 6, 1995, p. 21.

Lou Jones, "The Death Row Project," *Prison Life*, September/October 1995, p. 34.

David A. Kaplan, "Anger and Ambivalence," *Newsweek*, August 7, 1995, p. 24.

———, "Life and Death Decisions," *Newsweek*, June 16, 1997, p. 28.

Alex Kozinski, "Tinkering with Death," *New Yorker*, February 10, 1997, p. 48.

Peter Linebaugh, "The Farce of the Death Penalty," *Nation*, August 14, 1995, p. 165.

Stephen Markman, "Innocents on Death Row?" *National Review*, September 12, 1994, p. 72.

Tom Morganthau, "Condemned to Life," *Newsweek*, August 7, 1995, p. 19.

Tom Morganthau and Peter Annin, "Should McVeigh Die?" *Newsweek*, June 16, 1997, p. 20.

Ruth Morris, "Alternatives to the Death Penalty," *Witness*, September 1997, p. 18.

Richard H. Nicholson, "Is Capital Punishment Ever Ethical?" *Hastings Center Report*, July/August 1995, p. 5.

"The Place for Vengeance," *U.S. News & World Report*, June 16, 1997, p. 25.

Stephen J. Pope, "Compassion for a Killer?" *America*, November 9, 1996, p. 13.

Anna Quindlen, "The High Cost of Death," *Liberal Opinion Week*, December 5, 1994, p. 6.

Michael Radelet, "Poorly Executed," *Harper's Magazine*, June 1995, p. 21.

Robert Reno, "Death Penalty's Supporters Are in for a Shock," *Liberal Opinion Week*, December 5, 1994, p. 6.

Michael Ross, "Is the Death Penalty Racist?" *Human Rights*, Summer 1994, p. 24.

Stanley Rothman and Stephen Powers, "Execution by Quota?" *Public Interest*, Summer 1994, p. 12.

Joseph Sobran, "Death Penalty Deters Criminals," *Conservative Chronicle*, January 5, 1994, p. 22.

Thomas Sowell, "Defenders of Murderers Spring into Action," *Manchester Union-Leader*, December 13, 1994, p. 21.

Arlen Specter, "Congress Must Make Death Sentences Meaningful Again," *Human Events*, July 15, 1994, p. 14.

Bryan Stevenson, "The Hanging Judges," *Nation*, October 14, 1996, p. 16.

Michael Tomasky, "A Bronx Cheer," *Nation*, April 15, 1996, p. 5.

INDEX

ABOUT THE AUTHOR

Gail B. Stewart is the author of more than eighty books for children and young adults. She lives in Minneapolis, Minnesota, with her husband Carl and their sons Ted, Elliot, and Flynn. When she is not writing, she spends her time reading, walking, and watching her sons play soccer.